GOAN ECONOMY: AN ANALYSIS OF SELECT ISSUES

Edited by

Silvia Maria de Mendonca e Noronha
Professor & Head,
Department of Economics,
Goa University

Goan Economy: An Analysis of Select Issues
© Silvia Maria de Mendonca e Noronha
First Edition: 2014

© **Published by**

SIGNATURE STORE:
1st Floor, Ashirwad Bldg.,Near Caculo Island, 18th June Road,Panjim-Goa.
Tel: 2420677, 6647037, 6647038, Fax: 6647038
Email: *bbcbooks@rediffmail.com info@booksingoa.com*
Website: *www.booksingoa.com*

CACULO MALL:
Caculo Enclave, St. Inez, Panaji - Goa. Tel: 2233338/9

CANDOLIM:
Landscape Holiday Unit, Ground Floor, Near Dr. Dukles Hospital & Research
Centre, Aguada Fort Road, Candolim-Goa. Tel: 6519777, (M) 9860030339

DUBAI:
● Shop No.38 B, Jumaira Plaza, Jumaira Beach Road, Dubai.
● Madina Mall, Shop 29-A, First Floor, Qusais 4, Dubai.
P.O. Box: 211373, Tel: +971 527338555, +971 556001252
Website: *www.booksindubai* E-mail: *info@booksindubai.com*

ISBN NO.: 978-93-80837-97-0

Printed by Rama Harmalkar 9326102225

CONTENTS

I.   **Trends in the Employment Pattern in Goa**   1
Silvia Maria de Mendonca e Noronha

II.   **An Empirical Overview of the Impact of HIV/AIDS**   27
on Income and Employment.
Savio P. Falleiro

III.   **Labour Welfare and Job Satisfaction: A Comparative**   52
Study of Indian Pharmaceutical Companies and
Multinational Pharmaceutical Companies in Goa'.
Christina De Souza

IV.   **Market Dynamics and Marketing Constraints-A Study**   79
of Marketing Problems of the Pharmaceutical
Companies Registered in Goa.
Anna Rovina F. Fernandes

V.   **A Critical Evaluation of ICDS (Integrated Child**   105
Development Services) Programme in Goa.
Agnela Dias

VI.   **Socio-Economic Impact of Trade Unions at**   129
Selected Units in Goa
Blanche Fernandes e Mascarenhas

VII.   ***Product Profile and Market Analysis of the***   148
Pharmaceutical Companies Registered in Goa.
Anna Rovina F. Fernandes and Silvia M de
Mendonca e Noronha

VIII.   **Problems of Women in Selected Industries**   167
in Industrial Estates in Goa.
Nirmala De Abreu

LIST OF CONTRIBUTORS

Dr. Agnela A.D. Dias, Associate Professor of Economics, Government College of Arts, Science and Commerce, Sanquelim- Goa.
e-mail: agnelaangelina@gmail.com

Dr. Anna Rovina Fernandes, Assistant Professor of Economics, Carmel College for Women, Nuvem-Goa.
e-mail:ann_rovina@rediffmail.com

Dr. Blanche R.C.S. Fernandes e Mascarenhas, Associate Professor and Head, Department of Economics, St. Xavier's College, Goa.
e-mail: blanonymas@yahoo.com

Dr. Christina De Souza, Associate Professor of Economics, Government College of Arts, Science and Commerce, Khandola-Marcela-Goa.
e-mail: christinadesouza5@gmail.com

Dr. Nirmala De Abreu, Associate Professor of Economics, Department of Economics, Govt College of Arts and Commerce, Pernem, Goa.
e-mail: ndja@rediffmail.com

Dr. Savio P. Falleiro, Associate Professor and Head, Department of Economics, Rosary College of Commerce and Arts, Navelim, Goa.
e-mail: falleirosavio@rediffmail.com

Dr. Silvia M. De Mendonca e Noronha, Professor and Head, Department of Economics, Goa University.
e-mail: silvia29470@yahoo.co.in

PREFACE

Not many books have been written on the Goan Economy. This book is a collection of research articles written by research scholars, who have worked on various issues pertaining to the Goan Economy. Since this was valuable research carried out by the researchers, we felt it appropriate to publish the same in an edited book, which would make all the research articles available in one place, for future research or plain reading, for those interested in the issues discussed therein.

To begin with we have a research article on the,' Trends in The Employment Pattern in Goa'. In this article I have attempted to study the trends in the employment pattern in Goa, in the post-liberation period. Based on the trends an attempt is made to explain the nature of economic development in Goa.

Dr. Savio Falleiro's article on, 'An Empirical Overview of the Impact of HIV/AIDs on Income and Employment', is an attempt at analysing empirically the impact of HIV/AIDS on income and employment of individuals and households in Goa.

Dr. Christina De Souza writes on, 'Labour Welfare and Job Satisfaction: A Comparative Study of Indian Pharmaceutical Companies and Multinational Pharmaceutical Companies in Goa'. The article is an attempt to draw a comparison between labour welfare facilities provided, and the level of job satisfaction experienced by employees in Indian, and multinational pharmaceutical companies in Goa.

Dr. Anna Rovina F. Fernandes' research article is on, 'Market Dynamics and Marketing Constraints-A Study of Marketing Problems of the Pharmaceutical Companies Registered in Goa'. The main aim of this article is, to bring into focus the factors that inhibit the market potential of the pharmaceutical companies registered in Goa, due to the changes in the external, legal, regulatory and economic environment, and due to internal diseconomies which inhibits marketing efficiency.

The research article on, 'A Critical Evaluation of ICDS (Integrated Child Development Services) Programme in Goa," by Dr. Agnela Dias, highlights the shortcomings in the working of ICDS (Integrated Child Development Services) Programme in Goa.

Dr. Blanche Fernandes e Mascarenhas' article on, 'Socio-Economic Impact of Trade Unions at Selected Units in Goa', attempts to analyze the actual impact of trade unions both on social, as well as economic aspects related to workers, and society at large.

A joint research article written by Dr. Anna Rovina F. Fernandes and I on, 'Product Profile and Market Analysis of the Pharmaceutical Companies Registered in Goa', presents a comparative picture of the product profile and market standing, of the pharmaceutical companies registered in Goa.

The book ends with a research article written by Dr. Nirmala De Abreu on, 'Problems of Women in Selected Industries in Industrial Estates in Goa', highlighting the problems working women face, with special reference to those employed in industry in Goa.

I hope this book will be of use and prove interesting reading for those interested in studying Goa.

Silvia Maria de Mendonca e Noronha

1

TRENDS IN THE EMPLOYMENT PATTERN IN GOA

— *Silvia Maria de Mendonca e Noronha*

I. THEORETICAL BACKGROUND

India's pattern of structural change has been very different from that observed in the developed countries. In the developed countries, the decline of the share of agricultural GDP and the rise in that of the manufacturing GDP took place simultaneously, and only later did the share of manufacturing decline and that of services increase.

In India , the service sector has started increasing without the share of the manufacturing sector increasing much, as a result of which, the service sector has come to have the largest share in income. This rise to dominance of the service sector even before the economy has become highly industrialised has been called the 'excess growth of the tertiary sector' by Bhattacharya and Mitra (1990).

Ghosh (1991), points out that the different growth pattern of India as compared to that of the developed countries, is common to many other LDCs. He observed that the tertiary sector in LDCs in the process of development grows simultaneously with the primary and secondary occupations unlike in developed countries.

* *Professor & Head, Department of Economics, Goa University*

Reasons cited are (i) In developed countries, the high level of income stimulates the rise in tertiary sector, whereas in LDCs, expansion is partly due to the lack of availability of jobs in other sectors (ii) The tertiary sector occupations are highly capital intensive in developed countries as compared to LDCs.

Reynolds L.G.(2000), is of the opinion that, the shift of the workforce to the tertiary sector in the developed countries of the world may be due mainly to a rise in consumer incomes and living standards, which has permitted consumers to spend much more on education, health, entertainment and other professional services.

According to Clarke C. (1940), Kuznets S. (1957) and Fisher A.G.B. (1945), as economic development proceeds there is a movement of the working population from agriculture to manufacture and from manufacture to commerce and services.

Nafziger E.W. (2009), while quoting a WB study says that as countries develop, the output and labour force share in agriculture declines and that in industry and services increases.

Subramanian K.N. (1977), is of the opinion that an expansion of the tertiary sector does not necessarily imply a high level of economic development, as in India, where the tertiary sector has expanded, but the level of development continues to be low, due to inadequate expansion of the secondary sector. According to him, the main reasons for the overcrowding of the tertiary sector in India is due to the abundance of labour, shortage of capital and existence of a large amount of unemployment.

II. OBJECTIVES OF THE STUDY

- To examine the trends in the employment pattern in the primary, secondary and tertiary sector, and their main sub-sectors in Goa, for the period 1961-2001.

- To examine the nature of economic development of Goa, based on the employment trends.

III. TOTAL WORKFORCE IN GOA

We begin by examining the total workforce in Goa.

Table 1

Total Workforce In Goa, 1961-2001

YEAR	MALE	FEMALE	TOTAL WORKERS	TOTAL POPULATION
1961	147,036 (60%)(25%)	97,225 (40%)(16.4%)	244,261 (100%)(41.4%)	589,997 (100%)
1971	192,624) (76%)(24%)	61,851 (24%)(7.8%)	254,475 (100%)(32%)	795,120 (100%)
1981 (MAIN) (TOTAL)	234,975 (75.5%) (23.3%) 247,342 (69%)(24.5%)	76,272 (24.5%)(7.6%) 108,867 (31.4%)(10.8%)	311,247 (100%)(31%) 356,209 (100%)(35.3%)	10,07,749 (100%)
1991	294,759 (71.4%) (25.2%)	117,977 (28.6%)(10.1%)	412,736 (100%) (35.3%)	11,69,793 (100%)
2001	376,113 (72%)(28%)	146,452 (28%)(11%)	522,565 (100%) (39%)	13,43,998 (100%)

Source: 1. Census of India, Goa , Daman and Diu, Economic Tables, 1961, 1971, 1981. 2. Census of India, Goa, Economic Tables, 1991, 2001.

Note: 1. Underlined percentages are percentages of the figures in the respective columns, with the total population of Goa in the respective years. 2.Percentages not underlined are percentages of figures in columns 2 and 3 with that of column 4.

From the table we note in column 4, that there was an absolute rise in the total workforce from 244,261 in 1961 to 522,565 in 2001.

In terms of percentage in the 1961 census, the workforce formed 41.4% of the total population of Goa (refer table). In the 1971 census it declined to 32%, a fall of 9.4% points from 1961-'71, and in 1981, if only the main workers are considered, there was a further fall to 31%, a one percent point fall over the 1971 census figure. But if we consider the total workforce figures in 1981, there was a rise to 35.3%, a rise of 4.3% points over the 1971 census. However, as already explained earlier, when a comparison is made of the 1971 census data, with the 1981 data, we will consider only the main workers, so, there was a slight fall in the percentage of the workforce from 1971 to 1981.

We note that the fall in the percentage of the workforce to the total population of Goa, was rather sharp in 1971. This was largely due to the fall in the female workforce in 1971, due to the change in the definition of a worker in the 1971 census, that affected the female workers more. From 1971 to 1981(main workers), there was only a marginal fall in the percentage of the total workforce to the total population of Goa, due to the expansion of employment opportunities.

Due to the change of the definition of a worker from census to census, the figures of the total workforce in the censuses, do not always indicate the real situation about the trends of the size of the workforce. To avoid this difficulty as already mentioned earlier, many economists, often analyse the change in the male workforce only, which is generally not significantly affected by the changes in the definition.

In the 1981-1991 decade, the percentage of the total workforce to the total population of Goa remained the same. In 1991-2001 decade there was an increase in the percentage of the total workforce to the total population in Goa – an increase of 3.7% points. If we consider the period from 1961-2001, we find that the percentage of the total workforce to the total population of Goa has declined by 2.4% points.

Table 2

Aunnual Rate Of Growth Of The Total Workforce

YEAR	COMPOUND RATE OF GROWTH
1961-71	0.4%p.a
1971-81	2.03%p.a
1981-91	1.18%p.a
1991-2001	2.37%p.a

Source: *Derived from table 1.*

From the table we note that the annual rate of growth of the total workforce from 1961-'71 was 0.4% p.a. and from 1971-1981 (if the total Main workers are considered in 1981, to get a more realistic picture) it was 2.03% p.a. From 1981 – 1991 it was 1.18% p.a. and from 1991-2001 it was 2.37% p.a.

During the 1961-'71 decade , the annual rate of growth of the total workforce was very slow. This can be attributed to the sharp fall in the female workforce in the 1971 census, as a result of the change in the definition of a ' worker' in the 1971 Census, which affected the female workers more than the male workers, as already pointed earlier. In the subsequent decade i.e.1971-81 there was a rise in the annual rate of growth , even if only the Main workers are considered. From 1981-'91 there was a fall in the annual rate of growth of the total workforce in Goa. The 1991-2001 decade again saw a rise in the annual rate of growth of the total workforce in Goa.

IV. TOTAL WORKFORCE IN THE PRIMARY SECTOR AND IT'S MAIN SUB-SECTORS

In this section we consider the total workforce in the primary sector as a whole , as well as in the main sub-sectors i.e. in Agriculture Proper (AP) and in Other than Agriculture Proper (OTAP) . Agriculture Proper consists of workers employed as agricultural labourers and cultivators and other than agriculture proper consists of workers engaged in mining, quarrying, livestock, fishing, forestry, plantations, orchard, etc.

The following table shows the total workforce employed in the primary sector and its main sub-sectors from 1961-2001.

Table 3

Workforce Trends In The Primary Sector And It's Main Sub-Sectors

YEAR	TWF IN AP	TWF IN OTAP	TWF IN THE PRIMARY SECTOR
1961	142,096 (82.6)	29,997 (17.4)	172,093 (100)
1971	98,815 (78.7)	26,733 (21.3)	125,548 (100)
1981 MAIN	88,932 (72.6)	33,568 (27.4)	122,500 (100)
MARGINAL	35,511 (94.6)	2,027 (5.4)	37,538 (100)
TOTAL	124,443 (77.8)	35,595 (22.2)	**160,038 (100)**
1991 MAIN	91,812 (74)	32,049 (26)	123,861 (100)
MARGINAL	21,599 (93.5)	1,500 (6.5)	23,099 (100)
TOTAL	113,411 (77)	33,549 (23)	1,46,960 (100)
2001 TOTAL	86,201 (68)	41,040 (32)	127,241 (100)

Source : *Census of India, Goa , Daman and Diu, Economics Tables, 1961, 1971, 1981 and Census of India, Goa, Economic Tables, 1991, 2001.*

Note: *AP   - Agriculture Proper OTAP - Other than Agriculture Proper*

TWF - Total Workforce

1.The absolute workforce, as well as the percentage in Agriculture Proper has been declining from 1961-2001.

2. In percentage terms, the fall has been 3.9% points from 1961-1971, to 6.1% points

from 1971-1981 (Main workers), and from 1981 to 1991 (TW) it has been 0.6% points. From 1991-2001, it was 9% points. The fall was greater from 1991-2001. During this decade due to the construction boom, many agricultural lands were converted to non agricultural, probably resulting in this drastic fall in employment in this decade.

3. In Other than Agriculture Proper (OTAP), the absolute workforce shows a fall from 1961-1971, but a rise from 1971-1981 (Main). From 1981-1991 (TW), there is a fall in absolute terms and from 1991-2001, there was a rise in absolute terms.

In its percentage to the total work force in the primary sector, OTAP shows a rise of 3.9% points from 1961-1971, and 6.1% points from 1971-1981. From 1981-1991 (TW), there was a marginal rise of 0.6 points. From 1991-2001, there was a rise of 9% points. In percentage terms, OTAP has shown a rise from 17.4% in 1961, to 32% in 2001, a rise of 14.6% points.

Thus, from the above, we note that the total workforce in AP has been declining, both in absolute, as well as in percentage terms, from 1961-2001, whereas, in the case of OTAP, there has been a rise in absolute, as well as in percentage terms, from 1961-2001.

We conclude from the above observations, that in Goa, Agriculture Proper still continues to employ the bulk of the labour force i.e. 68% in 2001, but, the employment in this sub-sector is declining, unlike that in OTAP which shows a growing trend. So we conclude that, within the Primary Sector, the people are increasingly being employed in OTAP as compared to AP. In AP in Goa, the main crop grown is paddy, which is by and large for home consumption and therefore the remuneration is low, as compared to the remuneration in OTAP.

Table 4

Annual Rate Of Growth (%) In The Primary Sector And It's Sub-Sectors

YEAR	1961-'71	1971-'81	1981-'91	1991-2001
PRIMARY SECTOR	-3.10	-0.2	-0.8	-1.5
AP	-3.6	-1	-0.9	-2.7
OTAP	-1.1	2.3	-0.5	2

Source: Figures arrived at, from the data available in Table 3
Note: AP= Agriculture Proper OTAP=Other Than Agriculture Proper

From the table we note that the annual rate of growth in AP has been falling from the decade 1961-'71 to 1991-2001, whereas that of OTAP has shown a negative growth in two decades , namely, 1961-'71 and 1981-'91 , but a positive growth in the decades 1971-'81 and 1991-'2001. We can thus conclude that, there was a definite shift of the workforce from Agriculture Proper to Other Than Agriculture Proper within the Primary Sector, from 1961-2001.

Main findings of tables 3 and 4

The total workforce in the primary sector shows a steady fall from 1961-2001, both in absolute terms and in percentage terms.

The absolute workforce, as well as the percentage of the total workforce in AP, has been declining during this period.

OTAP shows a fall in absolute terms in alternate decades, but a steady rise in percentage terms from 1961-2001.

From the above we conclude that in Goa, though AP still continues to employ the bulk of the labour force in the primary sector, i.e 68% in 2001, the employment in this sub-sector is declining unlike that in OTAP which shows a growing trend.

V. TRENDS IN THE TOTAL WORKFORCE IN THE SECONDARY SECTOR IN GOA

Goa under the Portuguese rule was largely an import oriented economy. This probably explains why the industrial sector in Goa, was almost non- existent. Even as late as 1940, there was not a single industry in the modern sense of the term. Mining was considered as an industry, though it did not undertake industrial activity in the strict sense of the term.

There were some industries subsidiary to mining like building and repair of barges, besides, there were also some small scale and cottage industries like basket making, making of bamboo mats, coconut/cashew distillation, sugarcane juice extraction, solvent extraction of oil cakes, salt extraction, rice milling, coir industry, canning and cashew nut industry. Some of these industries existed even prior to the advent of the Portuguese in Goa. Of these industries, the cashewnut industry and the canning industry earned some income for Goa from exports.

With Liberation in 1961, there was an all out effort made to set up industries in Goa. Goa had already missed out on two five year plans and it had to make up for this loss of time and finance which the other states benefited from. So a Planning Board was set up by the Government of Goa, Daman and Diu to give a boost to industry. To build up the infrastructure needed for industry, the government set up the GDDIDC (Goa, Daman and Diu Industrial Development Corporation). This Corporation was instrumental in setting up the industrial estates in Goa, with the first one being set up in 1966 in Corlim. Subsequently several industrial estates were set up in Tivim, Pilerne, Kundaim, Verna, San Jose De Areal, Tuem etc., thus giving a boost to industrial development in the region. The Government of India also identified Goa, Daman and Diu as industrially backward, thus encouraging industries to be set up in Goa by making loans available at lower rates of interest and also declaring a tax holiday for five years, for those who set up industry in Goa. This encouraged the setting up of many industries in Goa.

The setting up of the Goa Small Industries Development Corporation (GSIDC), the Goa Handicrafts and Rural Small Scale Industries Development Corporation (GHRSSIDC) and banking and non –financial banking institutions such as the Economic Development Corporation (EDC) have also helped in the industrial progress of the State.

Table 5

Workforce Trends In The Secondary Sector And It's Main Sub-Sectors

YEAR	MPSR	CONSTRUCT IONS	SECONDARY SECTOR	TOTAL WORKERS IN GOA
1961	18,350 (83%)	3,741 (17%)	22,091 (100%)(9%)	244,261 (100%)
1971	30,712 (73%)	11,338 (27%)	42,050 (100%)(16.5%)	254,475 (100%)
1981	49,530(74%)	17,682 (26%)	67,210 (100%)(19%)	356,209 (100%)
1991	61,506 (71%)	25,621 (29%)	87,127 (100%)(21%)	412,736 (100%)
2001	77,867 (62%)	46,901 (38%)	1,24,768 (100%) (24%)	522,565 (100%)

Source : *Census of India, Goa , Daman and Diu, Economics Tables, 1961, 1971, 1981 and Census of India, Goa, Economic Tables, 1991, 2001.*

Table 6

Annual Rate of Growth (%) in the Secondary Sector and it's Sub-Sectors

YEAR	1961-'71	1971-'81	1981-'91	1991-2001
SECONDARY SECTOR	6.65	4.3	2.6	3.6
MPSR	3.6	4.3	2.6	2.4
CONSTRUCTIONS	12	4.2	3.8	**6.3**

Source : *Figures arrived at based on the data available in table 5*

Main findings of tables 5 and 6

1. We notice a rise both in absolute as well as in percentage terms, in the workforce employed in the secondary sector from 1961-2001, but this rise has been rather slow with the exception of the first decade i.e.1961-'71.

2. The highest growth in this sector is in the first decade soon after Liberation. As on 1961, Goa did not have industries worthy of mention. Whatever industries were in existence were traditional in nature, providing limited scope for employment opportunities. It was with Liberation that a boost was given to this neglected sector in Goa, which led to an expansion of this sector, and creation of employment opportunities evident from the higher compound rate of growth of this sector as well as, the higher percentage of the total workforce in the secondary sector to the total workforce in Goa, during the first decade after Liberation .

To give a boost to industrial activity in the state, the government set up the IDC (The Industrial Development Corporation) in 1966. The IDC was instrumental in setting up the first two industrial estates in Goa, at Corlim, and at San Jose de Areal. This gave a boost to the setting up of many small scale industries in Goa, by providing them with all the infrastructure facilities needed by them. Various schemes were also available for the industrialists to start industries in Goa, as Goa along with Daman and Diu was declared industrially backward by the Central government. This resulted in the setting up of many industries in the post liberation period. Financial institutions like the IDBI, IFCI, MSFC, SBI and other commercial banks were instrumental in providing financial aid to the industries.

3. With regard to the sub-sectors, the percentage of the workforce employed in MPSR has shown a declining trend

by and large, though it still continues to employ the bulk of the labour force in the Secondary sector.The annual rate of growth of this sector also shows a decline from 1961-2001.

4. With regard to the other sub-sector i.e. Constructions, there is a rise in absolute terms of the workforce employed in this sector from 1961-2001. In percentage terms, there also appears to be a rise from 1961-2001, with the exception of the 1971-1981 decade.The annual rate of growth of this sub-sector was high in the first decade after Liberation, and then it picked up again in the 1991-2001 decade.

We thus conclude that Constructions as a sub-sector of the secondary sector has been providing comparatively more employment opportunities in the secondary sector than MPSR, from 1961-2001.

VI. TRENDS IN THE WORKFORCE IN THE TERTIARY SECTOR AND IN IT'S MAIN SUB-SECTORS

In this section we consider the Tertiary Sector as a whole, and it's main sub-sectors, and try to analyse the trends in the workforce in this sector for the 1961-2001 decade.

Table 7

Workforce Trends in the Tertiary Sector and it's Main Sub-Sectors

YEAR	TOTAL WORK-FORCE IN TRADE AND - COMMERCE	TOTAL WORK FORCE IN TSC	TOTAL WORKFORCE IN OTHER SERVICES	TOTAL WORK-FORCE IN THE TERTIARY SECTOR	TOTAL WORKFORCE IN GOA
1	2	3	4	5	6
1961	12163 - (24%)	14,300 (31%)	22.618 (45%)	50,082 (100%) (21%)	244,201 (100%)
1971	24676 (28.4%)	22,864 (26.4%)	39237 (34%)	86,877 (100%) 34(%)	254475 (100%)
1981	38,607 (30%)	25854 (20%)	84498 (5C%)	129,259 (100%) (36%)	356209 (100%)
1991	59, 110 (33%)	32,473 (18%)	97,088 (49%)	178,849 (100%) (43%)	412735 (100%)
2001	1,15,941 (43%)	45,868 (17%)	1,09,037 (40%)	2,70,846 (100%) (52%)	522569 (100%)

Source: *Census of India, Goa , Daman and Diu, Economics Tables, 1961, 1971, 1981 and Census of India, Goa, Economic Tables, 1991, 2001.*

Table 8

Annual Rate of Growth (%) in the Tertiary Sector and it's Sub-Sectors

YEAR	T&C	TSC	OS	TOTAL
1961-71	7	4	6	5.7
1971-81	4	1	5	4.05
1981-91	4.4	2.3	8	3.32
1991-2001	6.9	3.5	2.3	4.25

Source : Figures arrived at based on the data available in table 7
Note: TSC=Transport, Storage & Communications
OS= Other Services T&C= Trade and Commerce

Main findings of tables 7 & 8.

- The tertiary sector has grown both in absolute as well as in percentage terms from 1961-2001. As on 2001, it employed 52% of the total labour force in Goa.

- The sub-sector of Trade & Commerce has grown both in absolute, as well as in percentage terms, from 1961-2001.

- From the annual rate of growth figures, we note that this sector has overtaken the 'OS' sector in providing employment opportunities.

- The sub-sector of TSC has been growing rather slowly during this period in comparison to the other two sectors.

- The sub-sector of 'OS' has shown a significant fall in it's annual rate of growth in the 1991-2001 decade.

- From the foregoing tables we conclude that the tertiary sector is the biggest employer in Goa, and the sub-sector of Trade & Commerce has contributed the most towards this employment, in the 1991-2001 decade.

VII. INTER-SECTORAL SHIFTS IN THE WORKFORCE

In this section we examine the inter-sectoral shifts in the workforce from 1961-2001, and try to see which sectors have lost their workforce over the years, and which sectors have gained. This will enable us to know to some extent, which sectors have grown and therefore have been able to provide greater employment opportunities.

Table 9
Inter - Sectoral Shifts in the Workforce

YEAR	PRIMARY SECTOR	SECONDARY SECTOR	TERTIARY SECTOR
1	2	3	4
1961	172,093 (70%)	22,091 (9%)	50,082 (21%)
1971	125,548 (49%)	42,050 (17%)	86,877 (34%)
1981	160,038 (45%)	67,210 ((19%)	129,259 (36%)
1991	146,960 (36%)	87,127 (21%)	178,649 (43%)
2001	1,27,241 (24%)	1,24,768 (24%)	2,70,846 (52%)

Source : *Census of India, 1961, 1971, 1981, Goa, Daman and Diu, Economic Tables; 1991 and 2001, Census of India, Goa, Economic Tables.*

Note : Figures in brackets are percentages of the workforce in the respective sectors to the total workforce in Goa.

Table 10

Loss or Gain in the Percentage Sectoral Shares of the Total Workforce in Goa

DECADE	PRIMARY SECTOR	SECONDARY SECTOR	TERTIARY SECTOR
1	2	3	4
1961-'71	-21	+8	+13
1871-'81	-10	+4	+6
1981-'91	-9	+2	+7
1991-'01	-12	+3	+9

SOURCE: *Adapted from Census data of 1961, 1971, 1971, 1981, Goa, Daman and Diu, Economic Tables and 1991, 2001, Census of India, Goa, Economic Tables*

Main findings of Tables 9 and 10

From table 9 it is evident that in 1961, the Primary Sector had the largest workforce, both, in absolute number (1,72,093) as well as in percentage terms (70%) when compared to that of the other two sectors, namely, the Secondary and Tertiary Sectors. It was followed by the tertiary sector, which had an absolute number of 50,082 and a percentage share of 21% of the total workforce in Goa, indicating that Goa was by and large, an agrarian economy during this period.

The Secondary sector had the lowest absolute number of 22,091 as well as percentage share - that of 9%. From the table it is evident that as on 1961, Goa was largely dependent on the primary sector for employment, due to the under development of the remaining two sectors.

In 1971 (refer table 9) there was a marked change in the distribution of the workforce amongst the sectors. The primary sector which was the largest employer in 1961, showed a sharp fall in its share of the workforce from 1,72,093 in 1961 to 1,25,548 in 1971 in absolute number, and from 70% in 1961 to 49% in 1971 in percentage terms, thereby, showing a 21% points fall from 1961-'71 (Table 10). Simultaneously, the other two sectors, namely, the secondary and tertiary sectors showed a significant rise in their respective share of the total workforce in Goa (Table 9). The share of the secondary sector increased from 22,091 in 1961 to 42,050 in 1971, in absolute number. In terms of percentage, it increased from 9% in 1961 to 17% in 1971 thus, showing an increase of 8% points from 1961-'71 (Table 10). With regard to the tertiary sector, there was a rise from 50,082 in 1961 to 86,877 in 1971 in absolute number (Table 9). In percentage terms it increased from 21% in 1961 to 34% in 1971 - a marked increase of 13% points from 1961-'71 (Table 10). This shows that in 1971, with 10 years of Liberation there was a marked shift in the sectoral distribution of the workforce in Goa. The share of the primary sector declined not only in relative terms, but also in absolute terms, and that of other sectors showed a rise, thereby showing that with Liberation, the other sectors were developed, and the heavy dependence on the primary sector for employment decreased.

In 1981, it is observed in table 9, that once again there was a considerable drop in the absolute number as well as, in the percentage of the workforce engaged in the primary sector . This fall in absolute terms has been from 1,25,548 in 1971 to 1,22,500 in 1981 and in terms of percentage , it was 49% in 1971 to 39% in 1981, showing a fall of 10% points from 1971-'81 (Table 10). The other two sectors, namely, the secondary and the tertiary sectors, show a rise in absolute, as well as, in terms of percentage in the share of the total workforce in Goa from 1971-'81. In the case of the secondary sector , it was from 42,050 in 1971 to 63,886 in 1981 in absolute terms and from 17% in 1971 to 21% in 1981 in percentage terms (Table 9), thereby, showing a rise of 4% points from 1971-'81 (Table10). With regard to the tertiary sector, it was from 86,877 in 1971 to 1,25,159 in 1981 in absolute number, and from 34% in 1971 to 40% in 1981 in terms of percentage (Table 9), thus, showing a rise of 6% points from 1971-'81 (Table10). It is observed here, that the rise in both absolute , as well as, in terms of percentage in the share of the workforce by the Secondary and Tertiary Sectors, is lower during the 1971-'81 decade, as compared with 1961-'71.

In 1991, we observe in the table, that the primary sector shows a rise in the absolute number, from 1,22,500 in 1981 to 1,23,861 in 1991. In percentage terms however, it shows a fall from 39%in 1981 to 32% in 1991, a fall of 7% points from 1981-'91 91 (Table10). However, if the total workers figures are considered in 1981 and 1991, we note that there is a fall from 1,60,038 in 1981 to 1,46,960 in1991 in absolute terms (Table 9), as well as, a fall in percentage terms from 45% in 1981 to 36% in 1991, (Table 9), a fall of 9% points (Table10).

The Secondary Sector shows a rise in absolute terms from 63,886 in 1981 to 84,302 in 1991. In percentage terms too, there is a rise from 21% in 1981to 22% in 1991(Table 9), a marginal rise of 1% point only, from 1981-'91 (Table 10) . Again here, if we consider the total worker figures, we note that there is a rise in absolute terms from 67,210 in 1981 to 87,127, in 1991. In percentage terms too, there is a rise from 19% in 1981 to 21% in 1991 (Table 9) - a rise of 2% points (Table10).

The Tertiary Sector shows a rise in absolute terms from 125,159 in 1981 to 175,396 in 1991. In percentage terms too, it shows a rise from 40% in 1981, to 46% in 1991 (Main Workers) (Table 9), a rise of 6% points from 1981-'91 (Table 10). However, if we consider the total workers figure, there was a rise in absolute terms from 1,29,259 in 1981 to 1,78,649 in 1991. In percentage terms, there was a rise from 36% in 1981 to 43% in 1991, a rise of 7% points from 1981 to 1991.

In 2001, we observe in the table that the total workforce in the primary sector decreased in absolute terms from 1,46,960 in 1991, to 1,27,241 in 2001. We also note a significant fall in percentage terms from 36% in 1991, to 24% in 2001- a fall of 12% points (Table 10).

The secondary sector shows an increase in absolute terms from 87,127 in 1991 to 1,24,768 in 2001, and in percentage terms an increase from 21% in 1991, to 24% in 2001 (Table 9) - an increase of 3% points from 1991 to 2001 (Table 10).

The tertiary sector also shows an increase in absolute terms from 1,78,649 in 1991, to 2,70,846 in 2001, and in percentage terms an increase from 43% in 1991 to 52% in 2001- an increase of 9% points.

Thus from 1961-2001, the Primary Sector showed a fall in absolute terms from 1,72,093 in 1961 to 1,27,241 in 2001. In percentage terms too, there has been a fall from 70% in 1961 to 24% in 2001 (Total Workers), thereby showing a sharp fall of 46% points from 1961-2001. On the other hand, the Secondary Sector showed a rise in absolute terms from 22,091 in 1961 to 1,24,768 in 2001. In percentage terms too, it showed a rise from 9% in 1961 to 24% in 2001, a rise of 15% points from 1961-2001

The Tertiary Sector increased in absolute terms from 50,082 in 1961, to 2,70,846 in 2001. In percentage terms it also showed a rise from 21% in 1961 to 52% in 2001, a rise of 31% points from 1961-2001.

We can thus conclude from the above, that there is a definite shift of the workforce from the Primary Sector to the Secondary Sector and more to the Tertiary Sector from 1961-2001 in Goa.

We conclude from these tables that the migration of the workforce from the primary sector has been absorbed to a larger extent by the tertiary sector.

Table 11

Percentage Distribution of NSDP at Factor Cost at Constant Prices in Goa

Sr. No	Sector	1971-72	1981-82	1990-91	2000-01	2010-11
1	Primary	40.0	28	18	12	8.88
2	Secondary	12	30	34	36	37.81
3	Tertiary	48	42	48	52	53.32

Source: *Economic Survey of Goa of the respective years*

If we compare the percentage distribution of NSDP at factor cost at constant prices in Goa, sector wise, with that of the percentage distribution of the total workforce in the three sectors in Goa, we find a similarity between the two. The tertiary sector contributes the maximum both in terms of employment, as well as to the NSDP, both in 1991 and in 2001. This clearly shows that, the tertiary sector is growing the fastest in Goa. As figures for 2011 are not available with regard to employment, in the various sectors, but we have NSDP figures sector wise, from the table, we can safely conclude that in 2011 as well, the tertiary sector will be the one growing faster than the others, not only in it's contribution to the NSDP, but also in terms of employment.

VIII. INTRA-SECTORAL SHIFTS IN THE WORKFORCE

In this section we will consider the intra-sectoral shifts in the workforce. This will enable us to have an idea on, how the shifts in the workforce have taken place within the respective sectors, thus giving us an idea as to which sub-sectors are growing, and which are lagging behind .

Table12
Intra-Sectoral Shifts in the Workforce

YEAR	PRIMARY SECTOR		SECONDARY SECTOR		TERTIARY SECTOR		
	AP	OATP	MPSR	CONST-RUCT-IONS	TRADE & COMM-ERCE	TSC	OS
1	2	3	4	5	6	7	8
1961	1,42,096 (58%)	29,997 (12%)	18,350 (8%)	3,724 (2%)	12,163 (5%)	15,300 (6%)	22,619 (9%)
1971	98,815 (39%)	26,733 (11%)	30,712 (12%)	11,338 (4%)	24,676 (10%)	22,964 (9%)	39,237 (15%)
1981	1,24,443 (35%)	35,595 (10%)	49,530 (14%)	17,682 (5%)	38,607 (11%)	25,854 (7%)	64,500 (18%)
1991	1,13,411 (28%)	33,549 (8%)	61,506 (15%)	25,621 (6%)	59,110 (14%)	32,473 (8%)	87,066 (21%)
2001	86,201 (16%)	41,040 (8%)	77,867 (15%)	46,901 (9%)	1,15,941 (22%)	45,868 (9%)	1,09,037 (21%)

Source: Adapted from Census data of 1961, 1971, 1971, 1981, Goa, Daman and Diu, Economic Tables and 1991, 2001, Census of India, Goa, Economic Tables.

Table 12 shows the percentage, as well as the absolute number of the workforce engaged in the various sub-sectors in Goa. We observe from the table that in 1961, 'Agriculture Proper" had the highest percentage as well as the absolute number of the total workforce in Goa i.e. 58% followed by 'Allied Activities' in agriculture (12%); Other Services (9%); Manufacturing, Processing, Servicing and Repairs (MPSR), (8%); Transport, Storage and Communications (TSC), (6%); Trade and Commerce (5%) and Constructions, (2%), in that order respectively.

In 1971, the position underwent a change. The workforce in Agriculture Proper declined in absolute terms from 1,42,096 in 1961 to 98,815 in 1971, as well in percentage terms from 58% in 1961 to 39% in 1971, a fall of 19% points from 1961-'71. The workforce in Allied Activities in Agriculture too, showed a fall in absolute terms from 29,997 in 1961, to 26 ,733 in 1971 and in percentage terms from 12% in 1961 to 11% in 1971, thereby, showing a 1% point fall from 1961-1971. The remaining sub-sectors showed a rise in absolute terms, as well as in terms of their percentage share of the total workforce in Goa for the above period i.e.196i-'71 (refer to the above table). Of the remaining sub-sectors, Other Services and Trade and Commerce showed a comparatively higher rise in both absolute, as well as percentage share of the total workforce in Goa. The workforce in Trade and Commerce rose from 12,163 in 1961 to 24,676 in 1971, in absolute terms, and from 5% in 1961 to 10% in 1971, a 5% point rise in terms of percentage of the total workforce in Goa. With regard to 'Other Services', there was a rise from 22,619 in 1961 to 15% in 1971 in percentage terms.

In 1981, there was a fall in absolute terms, in the total workforce in 'Agriculture Proper' from 98,815 in 1971 to 88,932 in 1981 and from 39% in 1971 to 28% in 1981, in percentage terms. The remaining sectors showed a rise in absolute terms , as well as in percentage terms, with the exception of Allied Activities in Agriculture, which did not show any rise nor any fall in their percentage share of the total workforce from 1971-'81, and Transport, Storage and Communications, which showed

1

a fall in it's percentage share of the workforce during the above period (refer table).

In 1991, there was a fall in absolute terms, in the total workforce in Agriculture Proper from 1,24,443 (Total Workers) in 1981, to 1,13,411 (Total Workers) in 1991, and from 35% in 1981 to 28% in 1991, in percentage terms. Allied Activities in Agriculture, also showed a fall in absolute terms from 35,595 in 1981 to 33,549 in 1991 and from 10% in 1981 to 8% in 1991 in percentage terms. The remaining sectors showed a rise both in absolute terms as well as in percentage terms, in their share of the total workforce from 1981-'91.

In 2001, there was a fall in absolute terms, in the total workforce in Agriculture Proper from 1,13,411 in 1991, to 86,201 in 2001 and from 28% in 1991, to 16% in 2001 in percentage terms. Allied activities in Agriculture showed a rise in absolute terms, but remained the same in percentage terms. So too with MPSR and Other Services in the Tertiary Sector, that also show a rise in absolute terms, but no change in percentage terms. The remaining sub-sectors of Constructions, Trade and Commerce, Transport, Storage and Communications show a rise both in absolute, as well as percentage terms in their share of the workforce in the respective sectors from 1991-2001.

From 1961-2001, Agriculture Proper showed a fall in absolute terms from 1,42,096 in 1961, to 86,201 in 2001 and a fall in percentage from 58% in 1961, to 16% in 2001- a fall of 42% points. Allied Activities in Agriculture also shows a rise from 29,997 in 1961, to 41,040 in 2001, and a fall in percentage terms from 12% in 1961 to 8% in 2001- a fall of 4% points. MPSR shows a rise in absolute terms from 18,350 in 1961 to 77,867 in 2001, and a rise in percentage terms from 8% in 1961 to 15% in 2001- a rise of 7% points from 1961 to 2001. Constructions too showed a rise in absolute terms from 3,741 in 1961 to 46,901 in 2001, and from 2% in 1961 to 9% in 2001 – a rise of 7%

points from 1961 to 2001. Trade and Commerce showed a rise in absolute terms from 12,163 in 1961 to 1,15,941 in 2001, and from 5% in 1961 to 22% in 2001 – a rise of 17% points from 1961 to 2001. Transport, Storage and Communications too showed a rise in absolute terms from 15,300 in 1961 to 45,868 in 2001, and from 6% in 1961 to 9% in 2001 – a rise of 3% points from 1961 to 2001. Other Services showed a rise in absolute terms from 22,619 in 1961 to 1,09,037 in 2001, and from 9% in 1961 to 21% in 2001- a rise of 12% points from 1961 to 2001.

From the above we conclude that, there was a shift of the workforce from the primary sector to the tertiary sector in Goa from 1961 to 2001 . The sub-sectors of Trade and Commerce had a larger share of the workforce both in absolute and in percentage terms followed by Other Services, thereby implying that these two sub-sectors of the tertiary sector grew more than the others.

The following table gives a clearer picture of the loss/gain by the various sub-sectors

Table13
Loss or Gain in Percentage Intra-sectoral Shares of the Total Workforce in Goa

YEAR	PRIMARY SECTOTR	SECONDARY SECTOR			TERTIARY SECTION		
	AP	OTAP	MPSR	CONSTRUCTIONS	TRADE & COMMERCE	TSC	OS
1	2	3	4	5	6	7	8
1961-71	-19	-1	+4	+2	+5	+3	+6
1971-'81	-10.5	0	+3	+1.5	+2	-1	+5
1981-'91	-7	-2	+1	+1	+3	+1	+3
1991-2001	-12	0	+0	+3	+8	+1	0
TOTAL	-48.5	-3	+8	+7.5	+18	+4	+14

Source: *Adapted from the Census of 1961,1971,1981, Goa, Daman and Diu, Economic Tables and 1991, 2001, Economic Tables for Goa.*

When we examine the labour shifts in Goa during 1961-2001, it is clear that the sub-sector of 'Trade and Commerce' within the tertiary sector, is the biggest gainer of the workforce lost by the Primary Sector, followed by 'Other Services'. In the Secondary Sector, Manufacturing, Processing, Service and Repairs has gained marginally more than Constructions. The largest percentage of the workforce has moved out of Agriculture Proper from within the Primary Sector.

We also note that in the first two decades after Liberation Other Services gained a large part of the workforce, due to the expansion of Public Administration and Government by and large. In the 1981-91 decade, Trade and Commerce has been on par with Other Services, and in the 1991-2001 decade it has overtaken Other Services. This can be attributed to the promotion of Goa as a tourist destination, resulting in an expansion of tourism related activities, which resulted in an expansion of employment activities in this sub- sector.

CONCLUSION

- From the foregoing analysis of tables, we conclude that there has been a shift of the workforce from the Primary Sector, to the Secondary and Tertiary Sectors from 1961-2001.

- In this shift, the Tertiary Sector has been the biggest gainer, as from 1961-2001, the Secondary Sector gained by 15.5 percent points of the percentage loss by the Primary Sector, whereas the Tertiary Sector gained by 36 %
  points.

- Thus we can safely conclude that in Goa there is a definite shift of employment in favour of the Tertiary Sector, and towards Trade and Commerce within the Tertiary Sector.

- We can thus conclude that we have in Goa as in the rest of India, excess growth of the tertiary sector.

- A growing tertiary sector is often considered a sign of economic development, but, if the tertiary sector grows more than the secondary sector, it is not a healthy sign of development, as in the case of Goa.

- According to Subramanian K.N. (1977), when he speaks of the Indian economy, he says that a certain reduction in employment in the tertiary sector and a corresponding increase in the employment in the secondary sector, should be evidence of real development of the economy of India. This is also true in the case of Goa.

References

Government of Goa, Economic Survey 1971-72, 1981-82, 1990-91, 2000-01, 2010-11, 2011-12, Directorate of Planning, Statistics and Evaluation, Panaji-Goa.

Census of India, 1961, Goa, Daman and Diu, Economic Tables.

Census of India, 1971, Goa, Daman and Diu, Economic Tables.

Census of India, 1981, Goa, Daman and Diu, Economic Tables.

Census of India, 1991, Goa, Economic Tables.

Census of India, 2001, Goa, Economic Tables.

Bhattacharya, B.B and Arup Mitra (1990), "Excess Growth of Tertiary Sector in the Indian Economy, Issues and Implications", Economic and Political Weekly, Vol.XXV, No.44, November.

Clark Colin, (1940), The Conditions of Economic Progress, Macmillan and Company, London.

Ghosh Arun (1987),' Winners and Losers of 1987-1988 Budget', Economic and Political Weekly Vol. XXII, No.12, March 21.

Kuznets ,Simon (1959), Six Lectures on Economic Growth, Free Press of Glenco, New York.

Reynolds L.G., (2000), Labour Economics and Labour Relations, Prentice - Hall of India Pvt.Ltd., New Delhi.

Kuznets ,Simon (1959), Six Lectures on Economic Growth,Free Press of Glenco, New York.

Subramanian, K.N., (1977), Wages in India, Tata McGraw-Hill, New Delhi.

Nafziger E.W., (2009), Economic Development, Cambridge University Press, New York.

2

AN EMPIRICAL OVERVIEW OF THE IMPACT OF HIV/AIDS ON INCOME AND EMPLOYMENT

— *Savio P. Falleiro**

I. INTRODUCTION

Ever since its detection almost three decades ago and having claimed over 25 million lives worldwide, HIV/AIDS has been a human and development catastrophe, particularly in developing countries where about 95 percent of the infected people live in. The severity of the AIDS epidemic in some countries has been such that according to the Red Cross and Red Crescent it should be classified as a disaster, i.e. an event beyond the scope of any single society to cope with (Foulkes 2008). According to UNAIDS (2010) there are presently an estimated 33.3 million HIV-positive (HIV+) people living around the world. India, with her dubious third rank globally vis-à-vis number of 'people living with HIV/AIDS' (PLWHA), has between 2.2–3 million infected people, with adult HIV prevalence of approximately 0.29 percent (GSACS 2010).

Goa, the place where the present study has been conducted, the highest per-capita income State in India, known internationally for her pristine coastline and tourism-centricity, has been considered by National Aids Control Organization (NACO) as a moderate HIV-prevalence State, with South-Goa district, one of only two districts of Goa, being amongst the high HIV-prevalence districts in India (The Times of India, 01/12/2008, 7). Bordered by high HIV-prevalence States of Maharashtra and Karnataka, there are an estimated 16,000 HIV+ people living in Goa; with about three new HIV cases detected each day at the Integrated Counselling and Testing Centre's (ICTCs) (GSACS 2010).

* *Associate Professor and Head, Department of Economics, Rosary College of Commerce and Arts, Navelim, Goa*

HIV/AIDS has multi-dimensional impacts including those of economic nature, at the individual/household (HH), sectoral/ occupation and macro/national levels. With regards to individuals/ HHs, the focal area of the present study, available literature in near unanimity points at the disproportionate burden faced by HHs from poorer and marginalised backgrounds; with the same being more vulnerable to the impacts than economically well-off and stable ones (Kadiyala and Barnett 2004, 1891). The poor thus run the risk of getting irreversibly impoverished (Medhini, Jain and Gonsalves 2007b, 1088).

Amongst the major economic consequences of HIV/AIDS on individuals/HHs, is its impact on income and employment. Employment is not only an economic necessity but an important source of dignity and self esteem, as well as a medium for daily social interaction with co-workers (Medhini, Jain and Gonsalves 2007a, 153). Drawing from NCAER study findings supported by UNDP and NACO, Pradhan, Sundar and Natesh (2006, 125) highlight that HIV HHs suffer income loss on account of HIV/AIDS in three key ways: a) currently working HIV/AIDS members are forced to take leave or be absent from work due to ill health; b) PLWHA dropping out of work force with worsening physical condition; and c) an employed caregiver in the family has to take leave to look after the infected members [see also Pradhan and Sundar (2006); and Pradhan, Sundar and Singh (2006)]. According to Booysen et al (2002) (in)direct income losses from HIV/AIDS amount to more than three times the average monthly income per capita of a HH in South Africa (see Canning et al 2006, 14). Incidentally, the implications of HIV/AIDS on income and employment affect adversely not only individuals/ HHs, but economic growth as well (Ojha and Pradhan 2006, xiv-xv).

II. OBJECTIVES OF THE STUDY

- To make an in-depth analysis of the impact of HIV/AIDS on income and employment pertaining to the HIV+ respondents;

- To make a comparative analysis wherever applicable with the matched sample of non-HIV/AIDS HHs; and

- To outline other impacts of HIV/AIDS on individuals/HHs with reference to income and employment.

III. RESEARCH METHODOLOGY

The study has been conducted on 200 HIV/AIDS HHs across Goa, each having at least one HIV+ member in the 18–60 years age group. The sample selection has been done through combination of non-probability sampling techniques as is usually the case with such studies involving hidden population, unknown universe and absence of proper/complete sampling frame. The sample has been drawn from amongst those whose HIV+ status was detected at the ICTCs in Goa; who are residing in Goa; who are living in HHs; who conform to the earlier mentioned age-group of 18–60 years; and who are able and willing to take part in the study. In terms of HHs, and factoring the numerous exclusions, the sample size is a figure '>5 percent' of those detected HIV+ at the ICTCs in Goa. The sample size is adequately comparable with other similar studies. The data collection was carried via in-depth interviews in 2009, through the (in)direct assistance of NGOs. Established ethical norms were followed right through the study.

The sample of non-HIV/AIDS HHs donning the role of control group was selected purposively on a 1:1 ratio with HIV/AIDS HHs. Factors given primary consideration for appropriate matching of the two independent samples' were: locale of the HHs, educational qualifications of the HH-heads, and socio-cultural background of the HHs. Two separate schedules were prepared for data collection; the same were adaptations of the questionnaires prepared by NCAER (2004; Pradhan, Sundar and Singh 2006).

The primary focus of the study is on income/employment of the HIV+ respondents' (one per HH) within the age group of 18–60 years, irrespective of whether presently employed or not in remunerative activity. With reference to the control group the focus is on one earning member per HH within the same age group.

IV. PROFILE OF SAMPLE HOUSEHOLDS

Select features of sample HHs' are as provided in Table 1.

Table 1 Comparative Profile of Sample HHs

(Figures in percentage terms given in brackets)

	HIV/AIDS HHS# @			NON-HIV/AIDS HHS ##		
	Sex of HH-head			Sex of HH-head		
	Male	Female	Total	Male	Female	Total
Age of the HH-head^						
20-30 years	6 [3]	13 [6.5]	**19 [9.5]**	6 [3]	2 [1]	**RS.**
31-40 years	49 [24.5]	28 [14]	**77 [38.5]**	34 [17]	14 [7]	**48 [24]**
41-50 years	32 [16]	15 [7.5]	**47 [23.5]**	53 [26.5]	15 [7.5]	**68 [34]**
51-60 years	20 [10]	17 [8.5]	**37 [18.5]**	42 [21]	10 [5]	**52 [26]**
Above 60 years	10 [5]	10 [5]	**20 [10]**	17 [8.5]	7 [3.5]	**24 [12]**
Educational qualifications of the HH-head						
Illiterate	27 [13.5]	47 [23.5]	**74 [37]**	37 [18.5]	33 [16.5]	**70 [35]**
Primary	13 [6.5]	10 [5]	**23 [11.5]**	32 [16]	5 [2.5]	**37 [18.5]**
Fifth-SSC	57 [28.5]	20 [10]	**77 [38.5]**	69 [34.5]	10 [5]	**79 [39.5]**
HSSC	8 [4]	2 [1]	**10 [5]**	10 [5]	0	**10 [5]**
Graduate	9 [4.5]	3 [1.5]	**12 [6]**	3 [1.5]	0	**3 [1.5]**
Post-Graduate	1 [.5]	0	**1 [.5]**	0	0	**0**
Others	2 [1]	1 [.5]	**3 [1.5]**	1 [.5]	0	**1 [.5]**
Earning category of the HH-head						
Salary-earner	36 [18]	10 [5]	**46 [23]**	50 [25]	4 [2]	**54 [27]**
Wage-earner	26 [13]	23 [11.5]	**49 [24.5]**	65 [32.5]	22 [11]	**87 [43.5]**
Self-employed	16 [8]	5 [2.5]	**21 [10.5]**	13 [6.5]	2 [1]	**15 [7.5]**
Not applicable*	39 [19.5]	45 [22.5]	**84 [42]**	24 [12]	20 [10]	**44 [22]**
Total annual HH income						
≤ Rs 50,000	60 [30]	68 [34]	**128 [64]**	19 [9.5]	22 [11]	**41 [20.5]**
Rs 50,001-1,00,000	33 [16.5]	9 [4.5]	**42 [21]**	60 [30]	12 [6]	**72 [36]**
Rs 1,00,001-1,50,000	11 [5.5]	3 [1.5]	**14 [7]**	35 [17.5]	8 [4]	**43 [21.5]**
Rs 1,50,001-2,50,000	7 [3.5]	2 [1]	**9 [4.5]**	31 [15.5]	4 [2]	**35 [17.5]**
> Rs 2,50,000	6 [3]	1 [.5]	**7 [3.5]**	7 [3.5]	2 [1]	**9 [4.5]**

Continued

Occupation of HH-heads						
Farmer/cultivator	1 [.5]	0	1 [.5]	2 [1]	0	2 [1]
Agricultural labour	1 [.5]	0	1 [.5]	10 [5]	1 [.5]	11 [5.5]
Construction/related work	10 [5]	3 [1.5]	13 [6.5]	31 [15.5]	8 [4]	39 [19.5]
Skilled/semi-skilled/non-agri. labour	22 [11]	3 [1.5]	25 [12.5]	35 [17.5]	1 [.5]	36 [18]
Service (govt. / private)1	21 [10.5]	9 [4.5]	30 [15]	29 [14.5]	6 [3]	35 [17.5]
Petty bus/small shop	7 [3.5]	5 [2.5]	12 [6]	7 [3.5]	1 [.5]	8 [4]
Small artisan in HH/cottage industry	0	1 [.5]	1 [.5]	0	0	0
Self employed / professional	3 [1.5]	0	3 [1.5]	1 [.5]	2 [1]	3 [1.5]
Truck driver/cleaner	5 [2.5]	0	5 [2.5]	4 [2]	0	4 [2]
Other kind of driver	4 [2]	0	4 [2]	8 [4]	0	8 [4]
Pensioner/retired	14 [7]	11 [5.5]	25 [12.5]	21 [10.5]	3 [1.5]	24 [12]
Domestic servant/house-maids	3 [1.5]	17 [8.5]	20 [10]	0	9 [4.5]	9 [4.5]
Rentier /house	0	1 [.5]	1 [.5]	0	0	0
Housewife	0	17 [8.5]	17 [8.5]	0	17 [8.5]	17 [8.5]
Unemployed	1 [.5]	0	1 [.5]	2 [1]	0	2 [1]
Sick, cannot work	25 [12.5]	16 [8]	41 [20.5]	2 [1]	0	2 [1]
TOTAL	117 [58.5]	83 [41.5]	200 [100]	152 [76]	48 [24]	200 [100]

Source: *Field work of Author*

Notes: ^*Mean age of HIV/AIDS HH head was 44.95 years*

   [48.42 years for Control group]

   #Average size of HHs: 3.77 members

   ##Average size of HHs: 4.48 members

   * Non-earning members on account of unemployment, sickness, being housewives, retired etc.

   @69.5 percent of the HIV/AIDS HH heads were HIV+ (74.36 & 62.65% of male and female-heads respectively)

The mean age of sample HIV+ respondents was 36.5 years. While 45 percent of the respondents were males, 55 percent were females. Majority of the HIV+ respondents at 58 percent were employed. In case of 21.5, 59 and 19.5 percent of the respondents, the HIV+ status was detected '≤1year', '1-5years' and '>5years' (back) respectively.

V. LIMITATIONS OF THE STUDY

- One limitation, common for studies like the present, is that, on account of the sampling techniques used there can be no definitive generalizations for the entire population.

- Though selection and use of the control sample has been followed by other studies as well[1],one can never be assured of ideal and perfect matching of samples'.

- Although in line with existing literature on the concentration of HIV/AIDS amongst poorer and marginalised sections, and also despite broadly reflective of the types of HIV+ individuals listed at the ICTCs, it is likely for the samples' in studies like the present one to appear skewed more towards those from the lower economic brackets.

VI. RESULTS AND DISCUSSION

1] Previous versus Present Employment of the HIV+ Respondents

Of the 200 HIV+ respondents, 47 percent who worked at the time of HIV detection were also working at present. While 30 percent who were working earlier were presently not on account of HIV/AIDS, 11 percent of those not working earlier were presently working to make up for fall in HH income and to meet rising expenses on account of HIV/AIDS to self or other member(s). Of the remaining, while 9 percent of the respondents never worked; 3 percent who were neither working at the time of knowing their HIV+ status nor are working presently were working in between but had to give up the job due to HIV/AIDS[2].

While less than a quarter of the respondents' at 24 percent did not have to change their job after knowing of their HIV+ status, the majority of 53 percent had to. If we exclude those not employed at the time (23 percent), the figure of those who had to change or quit the job becomes even higher at almost 69 percent. Of these, 57.5 percent had to change or quit due to being too ill to work, with another 14.2 percent getting dismissed from work due to the HIV+ status (see Table 2). In cases of dismissal from service[3] the value of lost earnings could be greater than the former since the period over which the HH does not have access to an individual's earnings is potentially longer (Mahal and Rao 2005, 584-5). It needs to be mentioned that leaving aside dismissal from service and the role played by discrimination, the poor health contributed by HIV/AIDS itself is the main factor responsible for the loss of employment and income. Things on the employment front can only deteriorate if one adds the role played by actual and potential discrimination. Discrimination is economically harmful as it has the potential to exclude qualified and able workers from the labour force, besides unnecessarily increasing the burden on the social security system (Medhini, Jain and Gonsalves 2007a, 152). Incidentally, pertaining to the present study, of those who had to change their job after knowing of their HIV+ status, while the majority (52.8 percent) never worked again, most of the remaining changed their job on one or two occasions, with one extreme case changing as high as 12 times. Close to 89 percent of those who had to change or quit their job received neither financial compensation nor any other benefit from their employer at the time of leaving. Of those who received compensation ranging from a paltry Rs. 500 to a high of Rs. 3 lakhs, the mean amount received was Rs. 49,318 (SD: 86,817). One reason for the majority not getting any compensation was that most were employed in the private unorganised sector, with 22 being illiterate.

Table 2
Job Changes of HIV+ Respondents

	Frequency	% of total sample HHs	% of those who had to leave job
Reason for leaving the job			
Too ill to work	61	30.5	57.5
Dismissed from work	15	7.5	14.2
Took VRS	3	1.5	2.8
Discrimination at workplace	1	.5	.9
Others	26	13	24.5
Sub-total	**106**	**53**	**100**
Those who were not employed at time of HIV detection	94	47	
Total	**200**	**100**	
Whether received benefits at the time of leaving the job			
No benefit	94	47	88.7
PF (Provident Fund)	5	2.5	4.7
Compensation	5	2.5	4.7
NA-own job	1	.5	.9
Others	1	.5	.9
Sub-total	**106**	**53**	**100**
Those who were not employed at time of HIV detection	94	47	
Total	**200**	**100**	
Number of times changed job after detection of HIV+ status			
1 time	25	12.5	23.6
2 times	13	6.5	12.3
3-4 times	6	3	5.7
5-7 times	3	1.5	2.8
8 -10 times	2	1	2.9
>10 times	1	.5	.9
Did not take up job again	56	28	52.8
Sub-total	**106**	**53**	**100**
Those who were not employed at time of HIV detection	94	47	
Total	**200**	**100**	

Source: *Field work of Author*

Pertaining to those currently working, with regards to certain categories, there has been some noticeable shift in the nature of jobs. While there has been a fall in number of agricultural and skilled/semi-skilled/non-agricultural labourers, with the latter also being reported by Pradhan, Sundar and Singh (2006, xxi), there was a rise of those in services, petty businesses/small shops and domestic servants. Incidentally, of the seven 'unpaid' housewives at the time of HIV detection, there were none at present, since all took up remunerative employment to supplement HH income.

That agricultural workers feel the adverse impact of HIV as the virus takes its course by reducing the attendance, productivity and earning power was well documented by a comparative study involving AIDS contributed sick members and healthy tea-pluckers in Kenya (Fox et al 2004). With regards to agricultural workers/agriculture vis-à-vis the present study, leaving aside that there were no agricultural workers presently employed in HIV/AIDS HHs though there were at the time of HIV-detection, that HIV/AIDS has some in\direct adverse bearing can be seen through a comparative glance in the position of the two study samples'. While in non-HIV/AIDS HHs there were 13 agricultural labourers/cultivators as HH-heads, with 27 HHs owning livestock and 54 owning plots of land including those used for plantation, the corresponding figures were lower at 2, 11 and 37 respectively for HIV/AIDS HHs. Adverse impacts faced by agricultural HIV/AIDS HHs have also been recorded by other studies like Barnett and Blaikie (1992) and Verma et al (2002).While certainly lack of assets in HIV affected HHs could be an indication of the level of poverty existing ante-HIV/AIDS, it is nevertheless likely, as field observations affirmed, that HIV/AIDS is one cause that 'fuels' the process of decrease in assets (Nielsen and Melgaard 2004, 44). As the present study showed: a) currently non-HIV/AIDS HHs were having more assets than HIV/AIDS HHs; and b) even if lesser assets were owned by HIV/AIDS HHs on account of pre-existing ante-HIV detection poverty levels, while non-HIV/ AIDS HHs built up their assets position subsequently despite earlier similar poverty-level background, HIV/AIDS HHs have been unable to do the same due to dwindling incomes and rising expenditures.

The rise in 'services' jobs and 'domestic servants' can be directly attributed to the following: a) in case of services, a number of HIV+ individuals have been provided employment by HIV/ AIDS associated NGOs; b) with regards to domestic servants the rise is on account of its appealing nature, especially for females, due to flexibility in work hours, availability of a minimum of one free meal, closeness to ones residence, unskilled nature of job and availability of free time[4].

With regards to income slabs of those who were working at the time of HIV-detection, are presently working or both (see Table 3), there has been a significant rise in the number of those unemployed and hence coming in the 'nil' income bracket. While there were 22 non-earning respondents earlier, the figure has gone up to 60 at present, with the percentage figures being 12.5 and 34.1 respectively. There is thus rise in unemployment post-HIV detection - the same which was also noted by the NCAER/ NACO/UNDP study[5]. With regards to the others working at present also, barring an inconsequential case, there were generally more individuals in each income slab for the earlier employment as compared to the present. The mean earnings at present[6] are also much lower at Rs. 2,856 per month (SD: 5,092) as opposed to Rs. 4,694 (SD: 8,568) at the time of HIV detection, this despite there normally being a periodical increase in earnings anywhere on account of rise in cost of living; earnings which were as high as Rs. 75,000 per month earlier, were only as high as Rs. 37,000 at present. In case of 51.1 percent of the respondents who ever worked, the earnings have become lower now; with the earnings of 15.3 percent not undergoing any change[7].

Table 3
Income Slabs of those Employed at the time
of HIV Detection and/or at Present

Per month income slabs of HIV+ respondents	No. of those employed at time of HIV-detection	% of those employed at time of HIV-detection	No. of those presently employed	% of those presently employed
Nil [not employed]	22	12.5	60	34.1
Up to Rs. 1000	21	11.9	16	9.1
Rs. 1001-2000	37	21	38	21.6
Rs. 2001-3500	35	199	21	11.9
Rs. 3501-5000	26	14.8	19	10.8
Rs. 5001-7500	14	8	10	5.7
Rs. 7501-10,000	8	4.5	2	1.1
Rs. 10,001-20,000	6	3.4	6	3.4
Above Rs. 20,000	7	4	4	2.3
Total	176	100	176	100

Source: *Field work of Author*

The primary explanations for the changes in current earnings as compared to the earlier ones are as follows: *a) earnings are higher now* – happens largely because of three reasons: firstly, some of those who were not working earlier are employed at present and hence their income slab shifts from 'nil' to positive brackets; secondly, those who have not changed their job, get their periodic increase in earnings; and thirdly, in a number of cases HH members have taken additional jobs; *b) earnings are lower now* - this primarily takes place because: firstly, some of those working earlier are not working now, and hence these move from positive income brackets to the 'nil' income bracket; secondly, there is often cut in earnings due to absenteeism, exhaustion of leave provided by the employer, inability to work full-time etc.; and thirdly, even where a previously non-working HH member takes up temporarily the job of the HIV+ respondent due to the latter's indisposition and/or inability, the earnings are lower on account of the formers inexperience and/or inappropriate temperament to the task at hand; *c) no change in earnings* - this happens despite number of years since HIV detection and in spite of gross salary amounts of employees in general going up periodically, since the same are neutralized in the case of HIV+ salaried individuals due to salary cuts on account of increased absenteeism. In case of wage-earners, while wage rates rise periodically, HIV+ individuals cannot always work as much as before, whether in terms of hours of work per day or days of work per month (due to HIV/AIDS contributed indisposition, weakness and incapability). Higher prevailing wage rate thus gets off-set with lesser working hours or days. It will not be wrong to say in relative terms, keeping in mind the regular rise in cost of living, earnings of over 66 percent of those employed, are lower at present than what they were at the time of HIV-detection[8].

2] Present Employment

As mentioned earlier 24 (12 percent) HIV+ respondents neither worked at the time of HIV detection, nor are presently working. Of the remaining, while 60 (34.1 percent) are currently not employed in any remunerative activity, 116 (65.9 percent) are, albeit with the unpleasant fact that mean earnings of about 52 percent of these were even lower than the official prevailing minimum wage rate which at the time was Rs. 103 per day. Unlike HIV/AIDS HHs which had 116 currently employed members, 99 percent of the control group HHs had earning members.

Majority of those working (50.9 percent) did not disclose their HIV+ status to their employer (see Table 4), with the figure increasing to 64 percent if we exclude the 24 respondents who were self-employed. In Maharashtra, the figure of those not reporting their positive status was 79 percent (Pradhan and Sundar 2006, vi). The present study revealed that over 83 percent of those who did not disclose their status acted so on account of fear of losing their job. Similar reasons for non-disclosure of status to employers, compounded by stigma and discrimination, have also been reported by ILO (2004) On an encouraging note though, among those in the present study who reported their HIV+ status, none experienced discrimination. However, though this is in contrast to an ILO study on HIV discrimination in India which found that approximately 6 percent HIV+ interviewees reported discrimination in the workplace (see Medhini, Jain and Gonsalves 2007a, 161), it is pertinent to note that the true extent of discrimination involving the present sample itself, could have been a positive figure, had the HIV+ status been revealed by all.

Table 4

Employment, Discrimination & Employer-support of Presently Employed HIV+ Respondents

	Frequency	Percent [for concerned categories only]
Number of HIV+ respondents currently working		
YES	116	65.9
NO	60	34.1
TOTAL	176	100
If currently working, does employer know of HIV+ status		
Yes	33	28.4
No	59	50.9
NA-Self employed	24	20.7
Total	116	100
If employer does not know of status, reasons for not disclosing		
Social discrimination and isolation	6	10.17
Fear of losing the job	49	83.05
Lowered prestige	4	6.78
Total	59	100
If employer knows of HIV+ status, any type of discrimination		
Yes	0	0
No	33	100
Total	33	100

Continued

If employer knows do you get any support from employer		
Yes	28	84.85
No	5	15.15
Total	33	100
If employer gives support, nature of support		
Reimbursement of medical expenses	2	7.14
Paid leave	7	10.71
Flexibility in work hours	2	7.14
Others [nutritional support, combination of above...]	21	75
Total	**28**	**100**

Source: *Field work of Author*

Incidentally, of those who reported their status to the employers, 20 were provided work by HIV/AIDS NGOs, and it is primarily these NGOs which were the employers providing 'support' to HIV+ respondents in a combination of ways including, provision of nutritional/medical support, flexibility of work-hours, paid-leave, financial advances etc. Amongst the remaining HIV+ respondents who reported their HIV+ status to the employers, four were domestic servants whose employers came to know of the status on account of regular absenteeism, indisposition, weakness or frequent visits to clinics and hospitals; three were drivers whose employers were in no regular contact since they resided abroad; and the rest were primarily unskilled/semi-skilled workers or employees in shops.

In the productive sector one immediate consequence of HIV/AIDS is the high level of absenteeism due to being increasingly afflicted with AIDS related illnesses and for taking a longer time away from work for seeking treatment (Rao 2000, 496). A study in Kenya substantiates the same, with even healthy workers not being spared because many take time-off to attend to health needs of infected family members who need care (ibid). Fox et al (2004, 321) highlight that during their last three years of life, tea-pluckers who ultimately were terminated because of AIDS, were absent from work almost twice as often as other tea-pluckers. That HIV/ AIDS has an adverse bearing on employment and income due to absenteeism caused by illnesses can also be seen in the present study which points at a big number of 52 (44.8 percent) currently working HIV+ respondents who lost income over the last one year due to the same; the corresponding figure being only 20 (10.10 percent) for the control group. Of the remaining, while 28 (24.1 percent) of the currently working HIV+ respondents were absent from work due to illness but did not lose any income, only 36 (31 percent) of those currently working were never absent from work. The corresponding figures for control group were 31 (15.66 percent) and a much healthier figure of 147 (74.24 percent) respectively.

The study found that the mean number of days of absence for all working members was 34.36 days for HIV/AIDS HHs, as against only 3.47 for non-HIV/AIDS HHs (see Table 5). According to Duraisamy et al (2003), on an average 43 workdays are lost in a six month reference period per HIV infected person (see Mahal and Rao 2005, 584). With reference to the present study, with regards to those who were sick and lost income due to absence, while the mean number of days absent was 65.04 days for the HIV+ working respondents during the last one year, it was only 18.05 for the working members from non-HIV/AIDS HHs. To compound matters, as a study in a sugar estate in Zambia revealed, besides AIDS contributing to significant man-hours lost, even on returning to work, infected workers often could not perform their duties satisfactorily (Rao 2000, 496). Among those members who were absent but did not lose income the figures were once again superior in case of the control group. Incidentally, while 210 days was the maximum number of days of absence due to illness in case of HIV/AIDS HHs, it was only 45 for non-HIV/AIDS HHs. Needless to say, details of absence mentioned herein are only those related to absence from work on account of illness; absence due to other reasons including religious/ marriage ceremonies have not been considered.

Table 5
Number of Days Absent in the Last One Year due to Sickness for those Currently Working

	HIV/AIDS HHs					NON-HIV/AIDS HHS				
	No. of HHs / members	Min	Max	Mean	SD	No. of HHs / members	Min	Max	Mean	SD
For all presently working members	116	0	210	34.36	44.18	198	0	45	3.47	7.82
For those absent and lost income	52	3	210	65.04	49.16	20	3	45	18.05	12.53
For those absent but did not lose income	28	2	60	21.57	13.89	31	2	30	10.48	7.09

Source: *Field work of Author*

Besides affecting HHs adversely as seen above, absenteeism (or even death) related to illness or care for sick family members can additionally cause organisational disruption, underutilization of equipment and use of temporary staff, all of which can adversely affect quality of products and services, and lead to decline in productivity and profits of organisations. HIV/AIDS caused illnesses and/or death lead to disorganisation within the company workforce due to factors like rising staff-turnover, loss of skills, loss of tacit knowledge gained from experience, declining morale and replacement costs (Sharma 2006, 131). Dixit (2005, 105) indicates that the costs of absenteeism and reduced productivity may be higher than the costs of eventual death itself.

Related to the days absent from work due to illness, is the amount of income lost due to the same. While amount lost in HIV/AIDS HHs was as high as Rs. 44,000, it was only Rs. 4,500 for non-HIV/AIDS HHs for the last 12 months. The mean earnings lost in case of only those losing income due to absence were Rs.7,210 and Rs. 1,620 respectively for the two categories of HHs. With regards to all working members taken together, irrespective of whether income was lost or not, the mean earnings lost were a substantial Rs. 3,232 for HIV/AIDS HHs and a paltry Rs.164 for non-HIV/AIDS HHs (see Table 6). Mann-Whitney U test conducted on all presently working members in the two categories of HHs showed there was a significant difference between the two samples' at the 0.01 level vis-à-vis income lost during the last 12 months on account of absence from work due to illness (U = 7179.5, Z = -7.529, p = .000). Incidentally, while Duraisamy et al (2003, in Mahal and Rao 2005, 584) had estimated that on an average in a six month reference period income lost per HIV infected person was roughly Rs. 3,000; Pradhan, Sundar and Singh (2006, xxii) reveal that the average income lost due to leave/absence over one year was Rs. 3,736.

Table 6

Income Lost due to Illness Caused Absence during the Last One Year

	HIV/AIDS HHs					Non-HIV/AIDS HHs				
	N	Min	Max	Mean	SD	N	Min	Max	Mean	SD
For ONLY those presently working and have lost income [Rs]	52	150	44,000	7,210	8611	20	150	4,500	1,620	1218
For ALL presently working members [Rs]	116	00	44,000	3,232	6771	198	00	4,500	164	619

Source: Field work of Author

In *fine*, when an HIV+ person who was absent from work due to HIV/AIDS contributed illnesses dies, temporary loss of income becomes a permanent loss, and funeral/mourning costs get additionally incurred (Gaigbe-Togbe and Weinberger 2003, 29). Unfortunately, besides dipping into scarce savings to meet high costs, families often get some costs 'compensated' by reducing investments in productive activities, like removing children from school to save on expenses and/or increase HH labour (ibid). The present study showed that 21 (10.5 percent) HIV/AIDS HHs, of which 17 (81 percent) were female-headed, withdrew their children aged ≤16 years from educational institutions on account of reasons like 'un-affordability', taking care of HIV+ members, and taking up of remunerative employment. The corresponding figure was nil for non-HIV/AIDS HHs.

3] MISCELLANEOUS

The primary focus of the study was on studying the impact of HIV/AIDS on income and employment of the HIV+ respondents, the same of which was highlighted above. Given below are some of the other fallouts of HIV/AIDS on individuals and HHs pertaining to income and employment.

i. Death of Earning AIDS Members [9]

Out of the total sample HIV/AIDS HHs, 77 (38.5 percent) HHs had members who had died of AIDS; in case of 70 HHs the members were earning members (33 working at the time of death, and 37 working earlier before HIV/AIDS made them to quit). The mean amount lost by these HHs[10] was about Rs. 63,500 per annum. The actual earnings lost are much larger than they appear given that they accumulate over several years when an individual dies, even under fairly conservative assumptions about working life spans (Bloom and Glied 1993; see Mahal and Rao 2005, 584). Notwithstanding the huge loss of HH income due to death of AIDS earning members, the loss becomes far worse when: i) the dead member was the only earning member, and/ or ii) there were two or more earning members in the HH who died of AIDS. That death caused by AIDS to working members can have an overbearing adverse economic impact on HHs' present and future can additionally be gauged from the fact that the overwhelming majority were in the economically productive age groups, with almost 74 percent being in the age groups of 18–40 years and about 90 percent in 18–50 years age groups. If we leave aside the five minors who died at very young ages, the figures become even higher at 81.4 percent and 98.6 percent respectively. The mean age of dead members was 33.56 years (SD: 11.07). Incidentally, in the context of 'demographic gift' of Bloom and Williamson (1998), death (and morbidity) caused by HIV/AIDS among those in prime working ages can cause a 'reverse demographic gift' thereby adversely affecting growth (see Mahal and Rao 2005, 590). Had it not been for HIV/AIDS contributed illness and consequent loss of full time employment and source of income, the HH income of at least 68 (34 percent) HHs would have been higher by an average of around Rs. 63,500 per annum. Needless to say, if this was the case, over one-third of the sample HIV/AIDS HHs would have been in higher income brackets. To put things in perspective, we need to note that, 147 (73.5 percent) sample HHs had their last total annual HH income '≤ Rs. 63,500' per HH.

ii. Loss of Income/Employment of Care-givers

HIV/AIDS often necessitates the assistance, services and/ or time of another individual – the caregiver (CG). With sample respondents coming mostly from lower income HHs and with full time care-giving being a luxury that most cannot afford considering that able HH members need to work to supplement HH income, care-giving whenever done is often only part-time. Majority of the HHs (54.5 percent) required a CG, either to take care of the HIV+ respondent or other HIV+ members. However, despite the need, 21 percent of the said HHs had to do without one. The mean number of months for which care-giving was required was 12.33 months. In HHs where there was the benefit of CGs, while in case of 53.8 percent of the cases it was the spouse who was the CG, in case of 10.8 percent each, it was the children or parents[11]. Majority of the CGs (61.29 percent) who were HH members or close relatives of the HIV+ individuals, were presently employed, with the majority being 'skilled/semi-skilled/non-agricultural labourers' and 'domestic servants' at 30.2 and 18.6 percent respectively. The study revealed that especially with regards to female HH members who double-up as CGs, being domestic servants to supplement HH income is a matter of choice, due to flexibility of work hours (on account of care-giving at other times). Incidentally, 9.7 and 4.8 percent of the CGs were minors and members >60 years respectively. While the youngest CG was aged 13 years, the oldest was 72 years. As in Dixit (2005, 111), HIV/AIDS can lead to increase in multi-generational HHs without the middle, income-generating, generation.

Pertaining to the present study, majority (85.5 percent) of the employed CGs who were HH members or relatives were from the economically productive age groups of 18–60 years, with the mean age being 35.19 years. Almost 79 percent of these CGs lost income due to absence from work on account of care-giving. The figure pertaining to income lost during the year by those HHs where CGs lost income due to care-giving, taken as a percentage of the total annual HH wage income was about 5.55 percent. Amongst CGs currently not employed, six were employed earlier, with four having to give up their job because of care-giving.

VII. CONCLUSION

The study has highlighted the severe nature of the impact that HIV/AIDS has on income and employment of individuals and HHs. Incidentally, amongst the sample HHs, there were some facing far serious fallouts and traumatic experiences than others. The crises was accentuated in HHs where: a) more than one earning AIDS members had died; b) two or more earning members including non-HIV members had lost their jobs during the course of last 12 months; and c) there was not a single member who was employed during the entire year.

Though HIV/AIDS has an adverse bearing on present HH income and employment, premature morbidity and mortality among sick individuals can lead to fall in future income and employment as well. The adverse fallouts faced by HHs can only worsen in years to come since: a) Many of those who are presently working are gradually becoming more sick and weak; coupled by insufficient medical treatment and nutrition due to 'unaffordability', they will themselves join the ranks of unemployed sooner than the non-infected, thereby reducing HH income further; b) Many of those in the study who lost employment/income, have lost it during the course of last 12 months; although HHs earned less income this year on account of the same, the figure was nevertheless positive - in the ensuing year(s) it will be nil; c) Children doing remunerative work or care-giving are deprived of sufficient education, which will deprive them of better earnings in the future due to insufficient qualifications and skills; and d) If we consider the possibility of the requirement for care-giving when present HIV/AIDS members need the same in the future there will/can be a further drop in HH income.

Lost earnings and increased expenditures have long-term adverse impact on HH savings and asset-holdings for a majority of HHs, especially since they are not covered by social security or health/life insurance (the present study revealed that only 2.5, 14 and 1 percent of the sample HIV/AIDS HHs had medical insurance, life insurance and Employee State Insurance respectively). Losing income and employment due to HIV/AIDS is a serious cause for concern not only because of being severely challenged by rising HH expenses (especially those medical-driven in nature), but also because for the purpose of covering deficits HHs depend disproportionately on borrowings and on the relatively unknown 'unrequited and/or unrevealed income' (UUI). The latter besides being informal and unreliable in nature unlike wage and/or non-wage income, as affirmed by on-field feedback, it includes amounts raised through the highly uncertain natured unilateral receipts and sometimes even via dubious and inappropriate means like gambling, petty crime and commercial sex.

In *fine*, with HIV/AIDS virtually paying havoc vis-à-vis income and employment, it is but necessary that the government, aided by NGOs, do make more focused attempts towards just and quick alleviation. Promoting capacity building, besides encouraging self-help groups and home-based entrepreneurship programmes can immensely help HIV/AIDS HHs in general and those headed by females in particular. Additionally, discrimination at workplace needs to be treated as a punishable offence. Termination of qualified and functionally capable PLWHA who pose no risk to others vis-à-vis HIV transmission should be strictly prohibited. Those currently employed who fail the above pre-conditions should be provided suitable alternative employment; if the same is not possible, an alternative job as compassionate employment should be provided as a right to HH members of those PLWHA that need to be terminated and/or released from employment.

*   *   *

Notes

1. Like Canning et al (2006); Fox et al (2004); and NCAER/NACO/UNDP (Pradhan, Sundar and Singh 2006).

2. Hereon, the 9 percent who 'never worked' and 3 percent who 'worked in between' will be clubbed together to constitute the never worked category since they were neither working at the time of HIV detection and nor are so at present.

3. Dismissal due to stigma associated with HIV and not because of illness related incapacity.

4. Useful for care-giving or resting if one is HIV+.

5. Showed an increase in percentage of unemployed PLWHA from 3.61 percent before test to 9.80 percent after test (Pradhan, Sundar and Singh 2006, xxi).

6. Excluding the 24 from the never worked category.

7. For the remaining 33.5 percent of those who ever worked, earnings have gone up at present.

8. Figure includes those whose current earnings are the same as before.

9. Only one person per HH has been considered for the purpose of study. If two or more have died details of the last person have been taken into account.

10. Excluding two whose details of income are unknown.

11. As per an ILO (2003, 3) supported study, CGs who looked after PLWHA were mostly spouses (60%), followed by parents (32%), children (6%) and siblings (2%).

References

Barnett, T., and P. Blaikie. 1992. *AIDS in Africa: Its present and future impact*. New York: The Guilford Press.

Bloom, D., and S. Glied. 1993. 'Economic implications of AIDS in Asia'. In David Bloom and Joyce Lyons (eds.), *Economic implications of AIDS in Asia*. New Delhi: Oxford University Press.

Bloom, D. and J. Williamson. 1998. 'Demographic transitions and economic miracles in emerging Asia', *World Bank Econ Rev*, 12: 419-55.

Booysen, Frikkie, Dingie van Rensburg, M. Bachmann, M. Engelbrecht, F. Steyn. 2002. 'The socioeconomic impact of HIV/AIDS on households in South Africa', *AIDS Bulletin* 11(1).

Canning, David, Ajay Mahal, K. Odumosu, P. Okonkwo. 2006. 'Assessing the economic impact of HIV/AIDS on Nigerian households: A propensity score matching approach', *Program on the Global Demography of Aging: Working Paper Series. PGDA Working Paper No.16*; http://www. hsph.harvard.edu/pgda/working.htm, accessed on 16 February 2008.

Dixit, A.P. (ed.). 2005. *Global HIV/AIDS trends*. Delhi: Vista International Publishing House.

Duraisamy, P. C., R. Daly, A. Homan, N. Ganesh, A. Kumarasamy, P. Karim, Sri Priya, C. Castle, P. Verma, V. Mahendra and S. Solomon. 2003. 'The economic impact of HIV/AIDS in patients and households in South India', *Draft,* Chennai: University of Madras, Department of Econometrics.

Foulkes, Imogen. 2008. *Aids epidemic - a global disaster.* http:// news.bbc.co.uk/2/hi/health/7474600.stm, accessed on 18 February 2011.

Fox, M.P, S. Rosen, W.B. MacLeod, M. Wasunna, M. Bii, G. Foglia and J.L. Simon. 2004. 'The impact of HIV/AIDS on labour productivity in Kenya', *Tropical Medicine and International Health,* March-9(3) pp. 318–324.

http://info.worldbank.org/etools/library/latestversion.asp?135887, accessed on 6 April 2011.

Gaigbe-Togbe, V. and M.B. Weinberger. 2003. 'The social and economic implications of HIV/AIDS', *African Population Studies Supplement B to vol 19;* United Nations - New York: Population Division, Dept. of Economic and Social Affairs.

http://tspace.library.utoronto.ca/bitstream/1807/5825/1/ep04034.pdf, accessed on 30 March 2011.

GSACS. 2010. *HIV/AIDS in Goa.* http://goasacs.nic.in/goa-HIV-data2010. pdf, accessed on 28 January 2010.

ILO. 2003. 'Socio-economic impact of HIV/AIDS on people living with HIV/ AIDS and their families', *ILO India Project: Prevention of HIV/AIDS in the world of work: A tripartite response.* New Delhi: ILO Publications, International Labour Office.

------- .2004. *Assessing the socio-economic impact of HIV/AIDS on people living with HIV/AIDS (PLWHAs) and their families in India.* New Delhi: International Labour Organization.

Kadiyala, Suneetha, and Tony Barnett. 2004. 'AIDS in India: Disaster in the making', *Economic and Political Weekly,* May 8, pp. 1888-1892.

Mahal, Ajay, and Bhargavi Rao. 2005. 'HIV/AIDS epidemic in India: An economic perspective', *Indian J Med Res* 121, April, pp. 582-600.

Medhini, Laya, Dipika Jain and Colin Gonsalves (eds.). 2007a. *HIV/AIDS and the law – Vol. I.* New Delhi: Human Rights Law Network [HRLN].

------- .2007b. *HIV/AIDS and the law – Vol. II*. New Delhi: HRLN.

NCAER. 2004. *Socio-economic impact study of HIV/AIDS: Questionnaire for HIV/AIDS households*. New Delhi: National Council for Applied Economic Research.

Nielsen, Jette, and Bjorn Melgaard. 2004. 'The economic and security dimensions of HIV/AIDS in Asia'. In Jai P. Narain (ed.), *AIDS in Asia: The challenge ahead*. New Delhi: WHO and Sage Publications India Pvt. Ltd. pp. 42-57.

Ojha, Vijay P. and B.K. Pradhan. 2006. *The macro-economic and sectoral impacts of HIV and AIDS in India: A CGE analysis*. New Delhi: NACO/ NCAER/UNDP.

Pradhan, B.K., and R. Sundar. 2006. *Gender impact of HIV and AIDS in India*. New Delhi: NACO/ NCAER/UNDP.

Pradhan, B.K., R. Sundar and Geetha Natesh. 2006. *Socio-economic impact of HIV and AIDS in Tamil Nadu, India*. New Delhi: NACO/NCAER/UNDP.

Pradhan, B.K., R. Sundar and S.K. Singh. 2006. *Socio-economic impact of HIV and AIDS in India*. New Delhi: NACO/NCAER/UND. Also available at:

http://data.undp.org.in/hivreport/India_Report.pdf

Rao, Digumarti Bhaskara (ed.). 2000. *HIV/AIDS: Issues and challenges – Part II*. New Delhi: Discovery Publishing House.

Sharma, Savita. 2006. *HIV/AIDS and you*. New Delhi: APH Publishing Corporation.

UNAIDS. 2010. *Global report: UNAIDS report on the global AIDS epidemic 2010*. http://www.unaids.org/globalreport/Global_report.htm, accessed on 20 January 2011.

Verma, R.K., S. Salil, V. Mendonca, S.K. Singh, R. Prasad and R.B. Upadhyaya. 2002. 'HIV/AIDS and children in the Sangli District of Maharashtra (India)'. In G.A. Cornia (ed.) *AIDS, public policy and child well-being*. New York/Nairobi: UNICEF Eastern and Southern Africa Regional Office.

LABOUR WELFARE AND JOB SATISFACTION: A COMPARATIVE STUDY OF INDIAN PHARMACEUTICAL COMPANIES AND MULTINATIONAL PHARMACEUTICAL COMPANIES IN GOA

— *Christina De Souza**

I. INTRODUCTION

The industrial world is becoming more and more competitive and globalized. In this scenario, people in the organization have suddenly occupied center stage. The success of any organization in the long run depends very much on the quality of its human resource (Sridevi, 2006). For building a stable and efficient labour force, it is essential to bring about a marked improvement in the conditions of workers' life and work. Labour welfare measures are an effort towards relieving the industrial workers from want, worry and the adverse effects of industrialization, by improving working and living conditions. The proper administration and implementation of labour welfare facilities plays an important role in fulfilling the economic, social, and psychological needs of employees. In satisfying these needs a favourable attitude towards the job can be developed. Job satisfaction is an attitude, which is the result of many likes and dislikes experienced while working in an organization. The provision of labour welfare facilities is one of the factors instrumental in promoting job satisfaction.

* *Associate Professor and Head, Department of Economics, Government College of Arts, Science and Commerce, Khandola-Marcela-Goa.*

Thus providing adequate labour welfare facilities and promoting job satisfaction assumes importance.

In a highly competitive world, pharmaceutical companies are in stiff competition with each other. Goa has emerged as a hub for pharmaceutical companies and is considered to be the sunrise industry. Goa has been able to attract big Indian and multinational pharmaceutical companies between the decade of 1993-2003 due to the tax holiday for Goa announced in the Union budget in the year 1993, which was further extended to the period up to 31-3-2004, as per section 80-IB (4) of the Income Tax Act (Salgaocar, 1992).

The present research aims to draw a comparison between labour welfare facilities provided and the level of job satisfaction experienced by employees in Indian and multinational pharmaceutical companies in Goa. It is an inquiry into the relationship between labour welfare facilities and the level of job satisfaction experienced in Indian and multinational pharmaceutical companies in Goa.

II. CONCEPTUAL FRAMEWORK

The concept of labour welfare has received inspiration from the concepts of democracy and welfare state. In a Resolution in 1947, the ILO defined labour welfare as "such services, facilities and amenities as adequate canteens, rest and recreation facilities, arrangements for travel to and from work, and for the accommodation of workers employed at a distance from their houses and such other services, amenities and facilities as contribute to improve the conditions under which workers are employed".

Report II of the ILO Asian Regional Conference (1947) defined labour welfare as a term which is understood to include such services, facilities and amenities as may be established in or outside the vicinity of undertakings to enable the persons employed in them to perform their work in healthy, congenial surroundings and to provide them with amenities conducive to good health and high morale.

The term labour welfare is very comprehensive and includes various types of activities undertaken for the economic, social, intellectual and moral benefit of the labour community (Kumar, 1994).

Labour welfare implies the setting up of minimum desirable standards and the provision of facilities like health, food, clothing, housing, medical assistance, education, insurance, job security, recreation etc. Such facilities enable a worker and his family to lead a good work life, family life and social life (Sarma, 1996).

In the broader sense labour welfare is a convenient term to cover all those aspects of industrial life that contribute to the well being of the workers. Labour welfare refers to any agency either statutory or voluntary, which aims at betterment of workers conditions (Srivastava and Devi, 1974).

Job satisfaction is derived from the Latin words 'satis' and 'facere' meaning 'enough' and 'to do' respectively. Job satisfaction denotes a process of gaining desired things at the desired level on the job (Chelliah, 1998).

Hoppock (1935) was the first industrial psychologist to provide the concept of job satisfaction in his classic work 'Job Satisfaction'. He defined job satisfaction as 'any combination of psychological, physiological and environmental circumstances, that cause a person to say – I am satisfied with the job'.

Locke (1976) regards job satisfaction as 'a pleasurable or positive emotional state resulting from the evaluation or appraisal of one's job experience'.

According to Ganguli (1994) job satisfaction is an attitude that results from a balancing and summation of many specific likes and dislikes experienced in connection with the job. It is the employees' judgement of how well the job on the whole is satisfying his various needs.

Job satisfaction is a general attitude, which is a result of many attitudes in three areas, namely specific job factors, individual characteristics, and group relationships outside the job (Blum, 1956).

Job satisfaction reflects the attitude, which results from a balancing, and summation of many specific likes or dislikes experienced in connection with a job. The mixture of feelings, attitudes and sentiments that contribute to a general feeling of satisfaction gives rise to job satisfaction (Joseph, 2001).

III. REVIEW OF LITERATURE

Goyal (1995) studied the awareness of labour welfare facilities and the relationship between labour welfare facilities and job satisfaction in her work titled *Labour Welfare and Job Satisfaction*. In her research a comparative study was made between six cotton textile industries in Punjab in the private, public, and co-operative sectors with a random sample of 350 textile workers. The study highlighted a positive relationship between labour welfare measures and job satisfaction. It was also revealed that the workers were satisfied with the labour welfare measures such as wages, housing facilities, and retirement benefits like gratuity and provident fund, and medical benefits. The maximum number of workers satisfied with these welfare facilities was from the private sectors. Moreover the percentage of workers who felt the absence of adequate quality of working conditions, and that the supervisors and co-workers did not help them in the hour of need were very low.

A study by Kumar and Yadav (2002) titled *Satisfaction Level from Labour Welfare Schemes in Sugar Factories in Gorakhpur Division*, examined the labour welfare schemes in the eight State government and private sector sugar factories of the Gorakhpur Division in Uttar Pradesh. Based on stratified random sampling, 240 workers were interviewed from these sugar factories, using a well-structured interview schedule. The results revealed that, overall the satisfaction level of workers from labour welfare schemes was low in both the private and State sugar factories. Further, the workers in both sectors ranked the four labour welfare schemes according to their importance, which fell in the following order housing scheme, medical scheme, followed by education and recreation schemes. However when a comparison was made between the respondents in the private and State sugar factories it was observed that worker's satisfaction level from welfare measures which affects work environment, is higher in the private sector sugar factories than in the State government sugar factories. Moreover satisfaction of workers from social security schemes, housing, medical schemes, education scheme, was higher for workers in the private sector sugar factories than the State government sugar factories. The study concluded that workers in State government sugar factories have less satisfaction from welfare schemes compared to those in the private sector sugar factories.

The study on labour welfare and job satisfaction was conducted by Agnihotri (2002). This study on *Labour Welfare Activities and Its Impact on Labourer Behaviour* found that job satisfaction and the different dimension of welfare facilities was significantly related.

Research study by Srivastava (2004) titled *Impact of Labour Welfare on Employees Attitudes and Job Satisfaction,* a comparative study was conducted on 200 workers in the private and public sectors of Kanpur city. The findings of the study showed that better labour welfare facilities have a deep impact on workers psyche. If the conditions of workers are improved and they are provided with good labour welfare facilities they will be more satisfied in their jobs. Welfare facilities work as incentives for workers. The study also found that there was a significant difference in the labour welfare facilities provided in the private and public sector. The public sector provides better facilities to their workers than the private sector. However welfare facilities like subsidized loan, canteen and safety of workers scored significantly higher in private sector than the public sector. Significant difference was also found in the job satisfaction experienced between private and public sector workers. The public sector workers were more satisfied with their jobs than private sector workers. Public sector workers experience job security and get promotion on the basis of kindness from authority, while private sector workers feel job insecurity and get promotion on the basis of hard work and performance. Moreover the private sector workers also received very good salaries and incentives than public sector workers.

Srimannarayana and Srinivas (2005) conducted a study titled *Welfare Facilities in a Cement Plant: Employees' Awareness, Utilization And Satisfaction* which analyzed welfare facilities provided by the private cement plant located in rural India, its administration and examined the extent of awareness, utilization and satisfaction of the employees with the welfare facilities. The sample of the study constituted officers in the personal department (management) and a random sample of 100 workers. The study found that the organization under study provided various welfare facilities (statutory and non-statutory) for the benefit of workers and their families. This reflects the commitment of the management towards employee welfare. Employees were familiar with the welfare facilities. They are making use of these facilities depending on their needs. Overall a majority of them were satisfied with these facilities.

Employee satisfaction is one of the most researched topics of organizational behaviour in India and abroad. Herzberg et.

al. (1957) determine that job content factors (motivators) such as responsibility, recognition, the nature of work itself, and job context factors (hygiene factors) such as pay and working conditions are responsible for the presence or absence of job dissatisfaction.

Sinha and Singh (1995) in their study on *Employees' Satisfaction and Its Organisational Predictors* on a sample of 248 managers and 1795 workers found that managers needed challenge at work, tension free life and freedom to do things in their own way, satisfying nature of the job, need to be recognized for one's efforts. On the other hand workers wanted promotion on time, good working conditions and better relationship at work including need to be recognized for one's efforts and satisfying nature of the job. Workers were found to be more satisfied than managers.

The study titled *The Impact of Technological Change on Job Satisfaction of Women Garment Workers in Developing Country* by Islam (2003) on 296 Bangladeshi women garment workers revealed that that the most important factors of job satisfaction in order of their importance were fair pay followed by work satisfaction, task significance, salary, supervision, bureaucracy, conflicts, information sharing, co-workers relation, benefits and promotion.

The study by Srivastava and Roy (1996) *on Work Adjustment and Job Satisfaction among Pro and Anti – Management Workers* on a random sample of 100 workers from Bharat Heavy Electricals unit in the city of Haridwar, Uttar Pradesh revealed that some dimensions of job satisfaction that is nature of work, senior – junior relationships, salary and working conditions are positively and significantly related to the attitude of the employees. No significant relationship was found between the rest of the dimensions of job satisfaction such as job security, advancement, functioning of the union, nature of corporate communication and attitude of employees.

Prabhu and Rodrigues (2003) investigated *Organisational Climate and Its Influence Upon Job Satisfaction: A Study in a Public Sector Organisation in India*. A stratified sample of 100 executives and non-executives from a public sector was selected. The dimension wise analysis revealed that employees perceived different dimensions of job satisfaction differently. Co-workers, resources, compensation and recognition were the dimensions which most of the employees reported high satisfaction. Training, supervision and management are the variables where they experienced low satisfaction.

The study by Joshi and Sharma (1997) on *Determinants of Managerial Job Satisfaction in a Private Organisation* on a random sample of 124 managers from a private sector organization located in Gujarat revealed that the best predictors of job satisfaction were job content and training. None of the 13 other independent variables studied are capable of influencing job satisfaction, such as scope for advancement, grievance handling, monetary benefits, participation, objectivity and rationality, recognition and appreciation, welfare facilities, support and warm communication, top management commitment, resourcing and recruiting, career/succession planning and performance appraisal.

In a study by Rahad (1995) on *Factors Related with Job Satisfaction of Village Extension Workers in Training and Visit System* on a sample of 240 village extension workers in Amravati division of Vidarbha region in Maharashtra State found that the contribution of hygiene factors to job satisfaction was more than the motivator factors. Among the various hygiene factors job security and advancement, adequacy of salary, physical conditions of work and social status attached to the job were positively and significantly related to the job satisfaction of the respondents.

Sharma and Sharma (2003) found that for job satisfaction of middle level mangers the predictor was monetary benefits.

The study by Rao, Sujatha and Chakravarthy (2002) on *Job Satisfaction of Employees, A Survey of LIC Employees* on a sample of 54 employees indicated that respondents were satisfied with their job. The study also found that among the factors contributing to job satisfaction majority of the employees were satisfied with the quality of training facilities, working conditions or environment, housing loan facility, and good or excellent relations with management. Further salary was highly associated with job satisfaction, followed by years of service. While promotion, satisfactory place of work and housing were not dominant attributes associated with job satisfaction. However salary was found to be the most important factor deciding the level of job satisfaction.

Joseph (2001) in his article *On Job Satisfaction Among Transport Employees* made a comparative study of the job satisfaction of employees in the private and public sector. The empirical study was conducted on a sample of 300 transport employees working in the private (180 employees) sector and public sector (120 employees) in the Kottayam district of Kerela. The findings pointed out that there was a significant difference between the public sector and private sector transport employees in their level of job satisfaction. Employees in the public sector were highly satisfied with salary and other allowances, social status, relationship with co-workers, working hours and relationship with passengers; whereas the private sector employees were highly satisfied in their relationship with co-workers, working conditions and relationship with passengers. The public sector employees are just satisfied with job security and trade union relations and their counterparts in the private sector were satisfied only with trade union relations. The satisfaction of public sector employees in the middle range was only in the case of management policies and working conditions. But the satisfaction of private sector employees in the average or middle range was for five variables namely salary and other allowances, job security, management policies, social status and working hours.

In a study by Katuwal and Randhawa (2007) titled *A Study of Job Satisfaction of Public and Private Sector Nepalese Textile Workers,* an investigation was made in comparing the job satisfaction of 372 workers in the public and private textile sectors in Nepal. The sample was selected on the basis of stratified random sampling. The results of the study determined that the workers in the public and private textile sectors experienced high dissatisfaction towards job facets, especially the facets of monetary expenditure of the organization, behavioural aspects of management, and employment policy of the organization. While comparing the workers in the public and private textile sectors, it was found that public sector textile workers were statistically more satisfied than their private sector counterparts with personnel policies, style of management, and welfare facilities. The private sector textile workers were statistically more satisfied with the duration of work, wages, job security, and training and development than those in the public sector. Both groups of workers had similar attitudes on the job facets such as autonomy in work, job interest, promotion, ability utilization, recognition, supervision style, colleagues, and physical facilities available in the work place.

From the review of literature it can be observed that there is a dearth of studies on labour welfare and job satisfaction in pharmaceutical companies and the relationship between labour welfare and job satisfaction. The present study is an attempt to fill this lacuna.

IV. SIGNIFICANCE OF THE STUDY

The study on 'Labour Welfare and Job satisfaction: A Comparative Study of Indian pharmaceutical companies and Multinational pharmaceutical companies in Goa' is the first of its kind undertaken so far in Goa. It can therefore be of immense use to employers and future researchers interested in this area. The study provides an insight into the labour welfare facilities provided by Indian pharmaceutical companies vis-à-vis multinational pharmaceutical companies in Goa. Moreover from the study the level of job satisfaction experienced by employees in Indian pharmaceutical companies and multinational pharmaceutical companies in Goa will also be realized. This will be of interest to the employers of these companies, as it will make them aware of the importance of providing labour welfare facilities, which facilities need to be improved upon, the extent of job satisfaction experienced by their employees and how satisfaction at work can be enhanced. The study will make the employers realize that the labour welfare facilities act as a panacea for the workers and will motivate them to work in a laudable manner. Furthermore the study can assist the employers arrive at policy decisions that will ensure efficiency in the enterprise, make workers work in the best interest of the company and retain their loyalties with the company. An organization's viability and potential for growth depends to a large extent on a satisfied labour force and this study can help industries realize this aspect.

Moreover the Government of Goa will become aware of the labour welfare facilities provided by the pharmaceutical companies in Goa and could take necessary steps to improve the facilities provided to the employees in these companies.

Future researchers interested in doing further research on labour welfare and job satisfaction would immensely benefit from the present research work.

V. OBJECTIVES OF THE STUDY

1) To compare the labour welfare facilities provided in Indian pharmaceutical companies and multinational pharmaceutical companies in Goa.

2) To measure the level of job satisfaction of employees in Indian pharmaceutical companies and multinational pharmaceutical companies in Goa.

3) To study the relationship between labour welfare facilities and job satisfaction of employees in Indian pharmaceutical companies and multinational pharmaceutical companies in Goa.

VI. HYPOTHESES OF THE STUDY

Ho1: There is no significant difference in the labour welfare facilities provided in Indian pharmaceutical companies and multinational pharmaceutical companies in Goa.

Ho2: There is no significant difference in the level of job satisfaction experienced in Indian pharmaceutical companies and multinational pharmaceutical companies in Goa.

Ho3: There is no significant relationship between labour welfare facilities provided and the level of job satisfaction of employees in pharmaceutical companies in Goa.

VII. METHODOLOGY OF THE STUDY

Sample of the study

For the purpose of the study the researcher selected four major industrial estates that house a large number of pharmaceutical companies in Goa. These industrial estates situated in the districts of North Goa and South Goa are Tivim, Pilerne and Kundaim, Verna industrial estates respectively. A total of five Indian pharmaceutical companies and five multinational pharmaceutical companies were studied from these estates. The population of the study comprised 841 employees working in the ten selected pharmaceutical companies in Goa (five Indian and five Multinational pharmaceutical companies). On the basis of proportionate stratified sampling, workers and managers were selected from these Indian pharmaceutical companies and multinational pharmaceutical companies in Goa. The sample represents 20 percent, of managers and workers in each of the selected pharmaceutical companies in Goa. The total sample of the study included 201 respondents, which is 24 percent of the population of the study. In Indian pharmaceutical companies (IPCs) the sample comprised of 115 respondents and that in multinational pharmaceutical companies (MPCs) included 86 respondents. Table 1 presents an overview of the sample of the study.

Table 1

Sample of the Study (N=201)

	Indian Pharmaceutical Companies			Multinational Pharmaceutical Companies		
	Managers	Workers	Total	Managers	Workers	Total
Males	20	44	64	29	27	56
Females	16	35	51	17	13	30
Total	36	79	115	46	40	86

Source: *Primary Data*

Instruments for data collection

Two instruments the Labour Welfare Inventory constructed and standardized by S. K. Srivastava (2002) and the standardized scale constructed by H.C. Ganguli and Dr. Rita Shresthya (1994) on Job Satisfaction were administered to the sample studied. The items in these scales were assessed using Likert's five-point rating scale ranging from "strongly disagree" (1 point) to "strongly agree" (5 point) for positive items and the reverse for negative items in the scales administered to the respondents.

The Labour Welfare Inventory (LWI) constructed and standardized by S. K. Srivastava (2002) consisted of eight dimensions namely education/training, recreation, medical, subsidized loans, canteen, housing, safety and others (related to the general well being of workers - uniforms, drinking water, toilets, leave facilities, workman's compensation, retirement benefits, rest rooms and bonus). All the forty-seven items were positive statements. The scores of the Inventory could be a maximum of 235 (47x5=235) and minimum of 47 (47x1=47) indicating provision of good labour welfare facilities and poor labour welfare facilities respectively.

The reliability coefficient of the Inventory using the test-retest method was: r=0.76 and the index of reliability was 0.84 indicating that the Labour Welfare Inventory is highly reliable and valid. The split-half reliability coefficient was 0.83 and the index of reliability was 0.89, which makes the Inventory reliable and valid.

The Job satisfaction scale by H.C. Ganguli and Dr. Rita Shresthya (1994) was answered in the first person. The Job Satisfaction Scale (JSS) included seven dimensions namely work itself, pay and other financial benefits, promotional and training opportunities, job security, supervision, colleagues/co-workers and company practices. Twenty-six items covered these seven dimensions of job satisfaction. The job satisfaction score of an employee was the sum of the scores of the alternatives the respondent checked for in the twenty-six items. The score range is 130 (26x5=130) to 26 (26x1= 26), indicating very high levels of job satisfaction to very low levels of satisfaction in the job.

The reliability of the scale using the test-retest method was: r=0.90. Odd-even reliability after using Spearman-Brown's correlation was: r=0.81. Validity of the scale was checked through the internal consistency method, that is, item analysis showing low correlations between items and high correlations between item score and total test score.

Method of data collection

Data was collected from both primary and secondary sources for the purpose of the research. Primary data was collected through field survey using interview schedules and questionnaire method. A total of 500 scales were administered to the respondents and 350 were received. Of these the number of fully completed scales was 201, while in the others some items were left incomplete. Thus only the completed scales (N=201) were selected for the analysis of data, in the research. The 201 usable responses represented 40.2 percent response rate. Secondary data was collected from books, journals, unpublished thesis, government reports and the Internet.

Statistical techniques used

The statistical analysis on the data collected included mean, standard deviation, students't-test, percentages, and Pearson's coefficient of correlation.

VIII. DATA ANALYSIS

Ho1: There is no significant difference in the labour welfare facilities provided in Indian pharmaceutical companies and multinational pharmaceutical companies in Goa.

To test the null hypothesis Ho1, the mean scores on the Labour Welfare Inventory (LWI) obtained from the IPCs sample (N=115) were compared with the means scores of the MPCs sample (N=86). The t-test was used to determine whether the difference between the mean scores of the two samples studied was significant enough to warrant attention. Table 2 presents the comparison of mean scores obtained on the LWI by IPCs and MPCs samples.

Table 2

Comparison of Mean Scores Obtained on LWI by IPCs and MPCs Samples

Company	N	Total	Mean	SD	t
IPCs	115	14953	130.03	25.162	7.92**
MPCs	86	14034	163.17	34.174	

** *Significant at the 0.01 level*
Source: Primary Data

The findings in Table 2 reveal that the respondents in MPCs have obtained a higher mean score (M=163.17) on the Labour Welfare Inventory than the respondents in IPCs (M=130.03). This implies that there is a difference in the labour welfare facilities provided in the IPCs and MPcs in Goa. Those in MPCs receive better labour welfare facilities than those in IPCs in Goa. To determine whether this difference is significant the t-test was conducted. The t-value obtained was found to be significant at the 0.01 level (t = 7.92, P<0.01). This implies that the labour welfare facilities provided by the MPCs are significantly different from those provided by the IPCs in Goa. The respondents in MPCs perceive the labour welfare facilities offered to them as significantly better than their fellow mates in IPCs. One possible reason could be that the MPCs due to their better financial standing compared to IPCs are able to offer superior labour welfare facilities to their employees, which in turn keeps the employees happy. The IPCs on the other hand, due to their financial constraints may find it difficult to make provisions for better welfare facilities. Moreover in the era of cut-throat competition and in the effort to retain labour, the MPCs may have realized the importance of labour welfare facilities, and provide these to a greater extent than IPCs in Goa. Consequently labour welfare facilities provided by MPCs to their employees are superior than those provided to their counterparts in IPCs. It can therefore be stated that the labour welfare facilities provided by MPCs is significantly different from those provided by IPCs.

Hence the null hypothesis Ho1 that states there is no significant difference in the labour welfare facilities provided in Indian pharmaceutical companies and multinational pharmaceutical companies in Goa is not accepted.

Studies have reported differences in labour welfare facilities provided in public and private sectors in India (Goyal, 1995; Kumar and Yadav, 2002; and Srivastava, 2004).

Difference between IPCs and MPCs on the Eight Dimensions of the LWI

Since the study found a significant difference in the labour welfare facilities provided by IPCs and MPCs Goa, it only seemed logical to further analyze and compare the difference between the IPCs and MPCs on the eight dimensions of the LWI (education/ training (Ed/Tr), recreation (Rec), medical (Med), subsidized loans (Sub loans), canteen (Can), housing (Hsg), safety (Saf) and others) and test the level of significance between them. Table 3 presents a comparison of the dimension wise mean scores on LWI for IPCs and MPCs. It also shows the t-values obtained on each dimension of the LWI that indicates the level of significance.

Table 3

Comparison of IPCs and MPCs Dimension-wise Mean Scores on LWI

Com-pany		ED/TR	REC	MED	SUB LOANS	CAN	HSG	SAF	OTHERS
IPCs (N=115)	Mean	13.95	11.44	17.19	9.77	9.19	9.57	23.05	35.85
	SD	4.63	5.09	3.34	4.33	3.28	3.72	3.41	6.73
t value		6.58**	5.28**	5.92**	6.48**	9.22**	5.98**	4.70**	5.34**
MPCs (N=86)	Mean	18.64	15.91	20.12	14.02	14.05	13.93	25.37	41.14

** *Significant at the 0.01 level*
Source: *Primary Data*

A glance at Table 3 shows that the respondents in MPCs have obtained higher mean scores on the eight dimensions of the LWI compared to those in IPCs. This implies that these dimensions of labour welfare offered by the MPCs are perceived as better than those offered in IPCs. The t-test was carried out to examine whether the difference between MPCs and IPCs on each dimension of the LWI is statistically significant. It was found that on all eight dimensions of the LWI, there was a significant difference at the 0.01 level. This indicates that employees in MPCs perceive superior labour welfare facilities and enjoy better welfare than their counter parts in IPCs.

Similar research findings by Goyal (1995); Kumar and Yadav (2002); Srivastava (2004); and Srimannarayana and Srinivas (2005) lend support to these results.

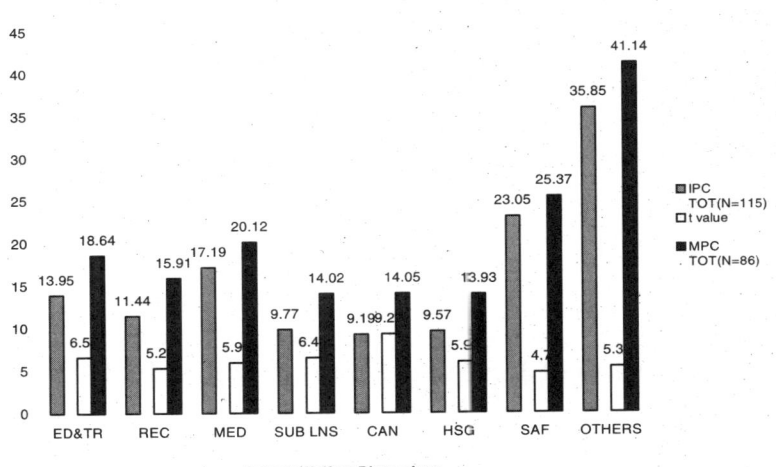

Figure 1: Comparison of Labour Welfare Dimension Means of IPCs and MPCs in Goa

Figure 1 compares the mean scores obtained by respondents in IPCs and MPCs on the eight dimensions of the LWI, indicating that labour welfare facilities provided in MPCs are perceived as superior to those in IPCs.

It can be summarized from the findings that the labour welfare facilities provided in MPCs (N=86) significantly differ from those provided in IPCs (N=115) in Goa. The respondents in MPCs identify significantly superior labour welfare facilities than their counterparts in IPCs. It follows that there is a significant difference in the labour welfare dimensions provided in Indian pharmaceutical companies and multinational pharmaceutical companies in Goa. The null hypothesis Ho1, which states that there is no significant difference in the labour welfare facilities provided in Indian pharmaceutical companies and multinational pharmaceutical companies in Goa, is not accepted.

Ho2: There is no significant difference in the level of job satisfaction experienced in Indian pharmaceutical companies and multinational pharmaceutical companies in Goa.

The testing of the null hypothesis Ho2 would reveal whether there is a significant difference in the level of job satisfaction experienced by the employees in IPCs and MPCs in Goa. To test Ho2, the mean scores on the Job Satisfaction Scale (JSS) for the IPCs sample (N=115) and MPCs sample (N=86) in Goa were compared, which would highlight any difference in their level of job satisfaction. To test if this difference is significant, the t-test was used. Table 4 compares the mean scores obtained on JSS by the IPCs (N=115) and MPCs (N=86) samples in Goa and shows the t-value.

Table 4

Comparison of JSS Mean Scores Obtained by IPCs and MPCs Samples

Company	N	Total	Mean	SD	t
IPCs	115	9024	78.47	16.17	9.076**
MPCs	86	8395	97.62	12.77	

**Significant at the 0.01 level.* Source: *Primary data*

From the table it can be observed that job satisfaction experienced by the respondents in MPCs is higher than that of those in IPCs, since the mean value obtained on the JSS by the MPCs sample (M=97.62) is higher than that obtained by the IPCs sample (M=78.47). To determine whether this difference is statistically significant, a t-test was conducted. The t-value calculated is significant at the 0.01 level (t=9.076, P<0.01). Thus, statistically, the difference in the level of job satisfaction experienced between the samples in the Indian pharmaceutical companies (N=115) and multinational pharmaceutical companies (N=86) in Goa is significant at the 0.01 level.

This indicates that the level of job satisfaction experienced by employees in the MPCs is significantly higher than that experienced by employees in the IPCs. The higher level of job satisfaction experienced in MPCs could probably be because the job facets offered by these companies may be better than that offered by the IPCs. Thus. the null hypothesis Ho 2 which states that there is no significant difference in the level of job satisfaction experienced in Indian pharmaceutical companies and multi-national pharmaceutical companies in Goa is not accepted.

Comparative studies on the job satisfaction of employees in private and public sectors have been drawn by researchers, which have shown that the employees in the private sectors are more satisfied with their job than their counterparts in the public sectors (Joseph, 2001; Srivastava, 2004; and Katuwal and Randhawa, 2007).

Difference between IPCs and MPCs on the Dimensions of the Job Satisfaction Scale

Various researchers have conducted studies to determine the job facets influencing job satisfaction and dissatisfaction (Herberzg, et. al., 1957; Rahad, 1995; Chelliah, 1998; Islam, 2003; Prabhu and Rodrigues, 2003).

The researcher went on to study the dimensions in the JSS that influence the level of job satisfaction of the respondents in the IPCs (N=115) and MPCs (N=86) in Goa. Table 5 presents the dimension-wise mean scores and the respective t-values.

Table 5

Comparison of IPCs and MPCs Dimension-wise JSS Mean Scores

Company		WI	P&FB	P&Tr	J Sec	Sup	CCW	CP
IPCs (N=115)	Mean	9.59	9.27	8.40	11.98	13.82	7.34	18.07
	SD	2.65	3.56	2.27	3.35	3.04	1.50	4.45
t value			6.69**	8.32**	8.21**	5.12**	7.57**	6.08**	6.32**
MPCs (N=86)	Mean	11.86	13.56	11.10	14.20	16.65	8.69	21.67
	SD	1.95	3.68	2.36	2.54	1.90	1.61	3.28

** *Significant at the 0.01 level*

Source: *Primary Data*

The results of Table 5 illustrate that the mean values on all the dimensions of the JSS are higher in MPCs than IPCs in Goa. This indicates that the respondents in the MPCs enjoy greater satisfaction on these job facets than their counterparts in IPCs. Moreover the difference between IPCs and MPCs on all these dimensions of the JSS namely, work itself (WI), pay and financial benefits (P&FB), promotional and training opportunities (P&Tr), job security (J Sec), supervision (Sup), colleagues and co-workers (CCW), and company practices (CP) are found to be statistically significant at the 0.01 level. This implies that the employees in MPCs in Goa (N=86) experience a significantly greater degree of job satisfaction on the dimensions of the JSS than their counterparts in the IPCs (N=115).

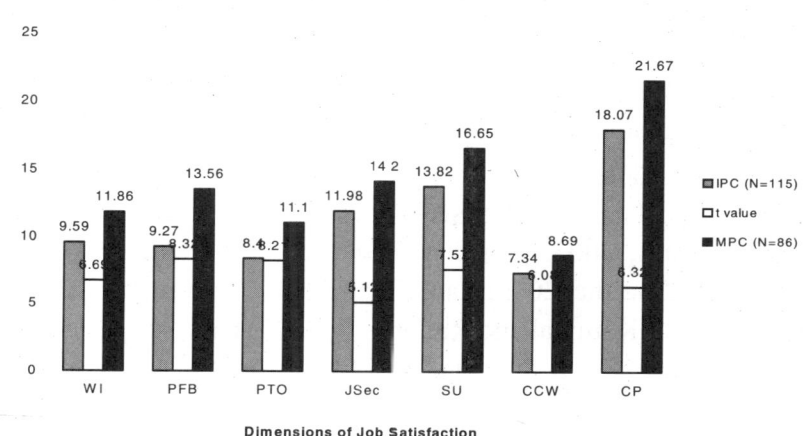

Figure 2: Comparison of Job Satisfaction Dimension Means of IPCs and MPCs in Goa

Figure 2 shows the differences in the mean scores of the IPCs and MPCs samples on the dimensions of the JSS.

The bar graph indicates that the MPCs (N=86) sample has scored higher on the dimensions of the JSS than the IPCs sample (N=115). Thus the respondents in MPCs are more satisfied with these job facets than their counterparts in IPCs.

This may be because the respondents in MPCs when compared to those in IPCs probably find their work more challenging, work with the latest technology, receive better monetary incentives, are sent on foreign assignments and trained regularly, promoted in accordance to their efficiency, enjoy a good rapport with their superiors, colleagues and co-workers, and are satisfied with the company practices such as appreciation of employees, personal growth of employees, provision of good working conditions. In IPCs the monetary incentives are usually lower, training is mostly in-house, limited communication with superiors, and company practices are shallow. Thus respondents in MPCs experience greater satisfaction on the dimensions of the JSS than the respondents in IPCs in Goa.

It should be noted that these dimensions in the JSS that are statistically significant include both the hygiene and motivator factors mentioned in Herzberg's two-factor theory (1957), thus implying that the level of job satisfaction in these companies is influenced by the hygiene and motivator factors. Herzberg's theory of job satisfaction (1957) supports the findings of this study.

Various studies by researchers (Ganguli, 1994; Sinha and Singh, 1995; Islam, 2003; Srivastava and Roy, 1996; Prabhu and Rodrigues, 2003; Joshi and Sharma, 1997; Rahad, 1995; Sharma and Sharma, 2003; Rao, Sujatha and Chakravarthy, 2002; Joseph, 2001; Katuwal and Randhawa, 2007) have supported the findings that pay and financial benefits, promotion and training opportunities, job security, supervision, and colleagues and co-workers, and company practices influence the level of job satisfaction of employees.

From the above discussion, it is realized that there is a significant difference in the dimensions of job satisfaction experienced by the respondents in IPCs (N= 115) and MPCs (N=86) in Goa. The null hypothesis Ho 2 which states that there is no significant difference in the level of job satisfaction experienced in Indian pharmaceutical companies and multi-national pharmaceutical companies in Goa is not accepted.

Ho3: There is no significant relationship between labour welfare facilities provided and the level of job satisfaction of employees in pharmaceutical companies in Goa. To test this hypothesis and determine the relationship between labour welfare and job satisfaction, Pearson's coefficient of correlation was used. Table 6, brings out the correlation between labour welfare and job satisfaction in pharmaceutical companies in Goa.

Table 6

Correlation between LWI scores and JSS scores for total sample (N=201)

	Job Satisfaction	Labour Welfare
Job Satisfaction	1.00	0.662**
Labour Welfare	0.662**	1.00

** *Correlation is significant at the 0.01 level (2-tailed)*
Source: *Primary Data*

The findings in Table 6 indicate a significant positive correlation between labour welfare and job satisfaction. Labour welfare is positively and significantly correlated with job satisfaction at the 0.01 level, wherein the correlation coefficient is 0.662. It implies that an increase in the labour welfare facilities in pharmaceutical companies in Goa will lead to a significant increase in the level of job satisfaction of the employees. As labour welfare amenities increases in the pharmaceutical companies in Goa the level of job satisfaction of their employees will also increase significantly. Thus if the pharmaceutical companies want to increase the level of job satisfaction of their employees then they need to pay attention to the labour welfare facilities provided to them.

Research studies that lend support to this finding include those done by Goyal, (1995); Agnihotri, (2002) and Srivastava (2004). Since there is a significant positive correlation between labour welfare and job satisfaction, the null hypothesis Ho3 which states that there is no significant relationship between labour welfare facilities provided and the level of job satisfaction in pharmaceutical companies in Goa is not accepted.

IX. CONCLUSIONS

The study drew a comparison between Indian and multinational pharmaceutical companies in Goa on the labour welfare facilities provided and the job satisfaction experienced by the respondents. Based on the findings of the study various conclusions can be drawn. The labour welfare facilities provided by MPCs is significantly different from those provided by IPCs. Labour welfare facilities offered by MPCs to their employees are significantly superior to those provided to their counterparts in IPCs. On all eight dimensions of the LWI there was a significant difference observed between IPCs and MPCs in Goa. The respondents in the MPCs perceived these dimensions to be significantly better provided than perceived by their fellow-mates in IPCs. Another observation made from the findings was the significant difference in the level of job satisfaction of the respondents in IPCs and MPCs in Goa. Those working in MPCs were at a significantly higher level of job satisfaction than those in IPCs. On all the seven dimensions of the JSS the MPCs sample experienced a significantly higher level of satisfaction than their counterparts in the IPCs. The study brought to light the positive significant relationship between labour welfare and job satisfaction in pharmaceutical companies in Goa. An increase in labour welfare is likely to increase the level of job satisfaction of employees in pharmaceutical companies in Goa.

References

Agnihotri. M. 2002. *Labour welfare activities and its impact on labourer behaviour.* PhD Thesis. Gurunanak University. Haridwar.

Blum. 1956. In Joshi, G. 2001. Occupational level and job satisfaction: A comparative study of public and private sector organizations. *Journal of the Indian Academy of Applied Psychology* 27 (1-2): 157-160.

Chelliah, C. 1998. Job satisfaction in fertilizers limited – A study. *The Journal of Institute of Public Enterprises.* 21 (1 and 2): 71-82.

Ganguli. H. C. and Shrethya. R. 1994. *Job satisfaction scales of effective management: Manual for managers and social scientists.* New Delhi: Concept Publishing Company.

Goyal, P. 1995. *Labour welfare and job satisfaction.* New Delhi: Deep and Deep Publications.

Herzberg, F. Mausner, B. Peterson, R.O. and Compwell, R. 1957. *Job attitudes: Review of research and opinions.* Pittsburgh: Pittsburgh Psychological Services.

Hoppock, R. 1935. *Job satisfaction.* New York: Harper.

ILO Resolution. 1947. In Goyal, P. 1995. *Labour welfare and job satisfaction.* New Delhi: Deep and Deep Publications.

Islam, M.N. 2003. The impact of technological change in job satisfaction of woman garment workers in developing country. *Management and Labour Studies.* 28 (4): 294-303.

Joseph, A. 2001. Job satisfaction among transport employees. *Journal of Psychological Researches.* 45 (2): 58-61.

Joshi, R.J. and Sharma, B.R. 1997. Determinants of managerial job satisfaction in a private organization. *The Indian Journal of Industrial Relations.* 33 (1): 48 – 61.

Katuwal, S. B. and Randhawa, G. 2007. A study of job satisfaction of public and private sector Nepalese textile workers. *The Indian Journal of Industrial Relations.* 43 (2): 239-248.

Kumar, S. and Yadav, S.S. 2002. Satisfaction level from labour welfare schemes in sugar factories of Gorakhpur division. *The Indian Journal of Economics.* 33 (329): 171-188.

Kumar. 1994. In Sarma, A.M. 1996. *Aspects of labour welfare and social security.* Bombay: Himalaya Publishing House.

Locke, E.A. 1976. The nature and causes of job satisfaction. In M.D. Dunnette (Ed). *Handbook of industrial and organizational psychology.* Chicago: Rand McNally.

Prabhu, M. and Rodrigues. L. L. R. 2003. Organisational climate and its influence upon job satisfaction: A study in a public sector organisation in India. *South Asian Journal of Management.* 10 (4): 13-22.

Rahad, B.G. 1995. Factors related with job satisfaction of village extension workers in training and visit system. *Finance India.* 9 (1): 141-142.

Rao, M.P. Sujatha, B. and Chakravarthy, P.M.G. 2002. Job satisfaction of employees: A survey of LIC employees. *Indian Journal of Marketing.* 32 (10): 28-34.

Salgaocar, D. R. 1992. Pharmaceutical Industry: 30 Years of Economic Development in Goa 1961-1991. In *Goa Chamber of Commerce and Industry.* Volume O.L.da Lapa-Soares. Panaji: Goa Chamber of Commerce and Industry.

Sarma, A.M. 1996. *Aspects of labour welfare and social security.* Bombay: Himalaya Publishing House.

Sharma, R.R. and Sharma, B.R. 2003. Organizational commitment and motivation among managerial staff. *Productivity.* 44 (2): 251-256.

Sinha, J.B.P. and Singh, S. 1995. Employees satisfaction and its organizational predictors. *The Indian Journal of Industrial Relations.* 31 (2): 135-147.

Sridevi, M.S. 2006. Role of HRD in the new economic environment. *Southern Economist.* 45 (7): 7-8.

Srimannarayan, M. and Srinivas, P.B.S. 2005. Welfare facilities in a cement plant: Employees awareness, utilization and satisfaction. *Prestige Journal of Management and Research.* 9 (2): 286-299.

Srivastava and Devi. 1974. In Goyal, P. 1995. *Labour welfare and job satisfaction.* New Delhi: Deep and Deep Publications.

Srivastava, S. K. 2002. *Manual for labour welfare inventory.* Uttar Pradesh: Parikchan Sansthan.

_____. 2004. Impact of labour welfare on employee attitudes and job satisfaction. *Management and Labour Studies.* 29 (1): 31-40.

Srivastava, S.K. and Roy, V. 1996. Work adjustment and job satisfaction among pro and anti – management workers. *Management and Labour Studies.* 21 (4): 237-240.

| 4 |

MARKET DYNAMICS AND MARKETING CONSTRAINTS-A STUDY OF MARKETING PROBLEMS OF THE PHARMACEUTICAL COMPANIES REGISTERED IN GOA

— Anna Rovina Fernandes*

I. INTRODUCTION

Small and medium firms, dominate the Indian pharmaceutical industry with significant contributior to the national drug production and employment. They play an important role in enhancing domestic technological capabilities in drugs production and have been instrumental in keeping drugs prices affordable for the Indian populace in remote rural areas. The rise of small firms in this sector has been facilitated by a set of strategic government polices implemented in the past decades like adoption of a process patent regime, relaxation granted from price control and industrial licensing requirement, reservation of items for exclusive production and preference in government procurement, etc. Since the 1990s, however, the regulatory regime for small firms underwent dramatic changes with withdrawal of most of the favourable policies and implementation of regulations like a long term product patent regime, withdrawal of exemptionfrom price controls, implementation of good manufacturing practices, etc. These new policies have a number of implications for the survival and growth of small pharmaceutical companies.

* Assistant Professor, Department of Economics, Carmel College for Women, Nuvem-Goa

The 1994-2004 decade witnessed an industrial boom in pharmaceuticals in Goa. The pharmaceutical industry blossomed in Goa during this period when the state was offered tax benefits as an 'industrially backward state'. Many small local enterprises along with big Indian and multinational companies set up their units in the state. The withdrawal of the tax concessions in 2004 led to adverse impact especially on the prospects of small scale pharmaceutical companies. Even bigger companies registered in Goa like Wallace Pharmaceuticals, which had planned to expand, decided to set up units in other states instead. Some like Dr. Reddy's Laboratories moved out of the State.

There has been a shift in the type of medicines being produced in Goa. Companies are using existing Goa units to produce export-based products, which can be quickly exported from Mumbai and products for domestic consumption have been shifted to places with tax concessions. Industrialists point that the ratio of domestic consumption to export also changed drastically, from 50:50 in 2005 to 20:80 in 2006.This shift led to closure of smaller units working on contract manufacturing basis. Only 15 of the 60 units, which had contract manufacturing deals, are still operational. The intensity of competition among the pharmaceutical companies in Goa is rapidly increasing and the market environment for the smaller local companies can be characterized as volatile, and complex.

II. OBJECTIVES AND METHODOLOGY

The objective of this study is to highlight the major problems faced by the existing pharmaceutical companies registered in Goa due to the changes in the external legal, regulatory and economic environment and due to their own limitations which inhibits their marketing efficiency. It discusses the existing national market environment in which the small and medium pharmaceutical companies in Goa operate. It conducts a SWOT

(Strengths, Weaknesses, Opportunities, and Threats) analysis of the registered pharmaceutical companies in Goa. Against this background, it examines the various problems faced by the companies in marketing of their products and discusses the implications and measures needed for the healthy growth of the industry.

The study covers the pharmaceutical companies that are registered with the Registrar of Companies, Govt. of Goa, under the Companies Act, and accordingly have their registered headquarters in Goa. The companies selected using convenience sampling method are: i) Wallace Pharmaceuticals Pvt. Ltd. ii) Cosme Farma Laboratories Ltd. iii) Kare Pharmaceuticals Pvt. Ltd. iv) Geno Pharmaceuticals Ltd. v) Merit Pharmaceuticals Pvt. Ltd. vi) Goa Antibiotics and Pharmaceuticals Limited. vii) Toyo Laboratories Private Limited.

Primary data has been collected by administering a questionnaire to the Directors/ General Managers/ Marketing Heads of selected companies and by using the personal interview method.

The study covers the time period from 2002-2007. Secondary Data pertaining to the companies for the period 2002-07, has been obtained from Annual Reports of the companies, obtained from the Registrar of Companies, Goa for the stated period.

III. OVERVIEW OF LITERATURE

In the context of new policy regime, technology and productivity are most important determinants of survival and competitiveness of pharmaceutical companies. Large as well small firms are required to urgently upgrade their internal sources of technology like expanding inhouse R&D activities, employing more skilled labour, investing in modern machinery and information and communication technologies, providing training to their technical manpower, etc. A study on R&D intensity of

223 Indian pharmaceutical firms for 1999–2000, has found that 139 firms had zero value of R&D intensity and another 47 firms had R&D intensity of less than 1 per cent of sales (Pradhan 2007). Together these firms account for 83 per cent of total firms under study, thus suggesting that a large number of Indian pharmaceutical firms do not engage in any R&D activity and the majority of those engaged spent a very small proportion of their turnover.

Literature on the aspect of critical success factors for the pharmaceutical industry lists several factors that are important for the healthy growth of the industry. The Indian Pharmaceutical Industry Report, developed by a team at ICRA, (1999), states that the rate of introduction of new products, and the marketing and distribution networks of companies will determine their future success. The new products in the Indian context are the outcome of process research, as opposed to basic research. According to the report, alliances, especially marketing alliances, will be the standard route to success. Significantly, many Indian companies which have entered into alliances to increase their geographic coverage, market reach and distribution network have assumed leading positions in the market.

Another study noted that infrastructure such as transportation, telecommunications, energy and education are the critical success factors for the industry.(Endersby 1999)

Giesecke studied the role of government in development of the pharmaceutical industry and concluded that direct government intervention is more likely to fail in achieving its goals. Successful; indirect approaches include enhancement of the already existing economic structure connecting academic innovations with market opportunities, availability of venture capital and professional business advice, possibilities for diffusion of knowledge, and competence of political bodies to distribute research money where innovations are most probable. (Giesecke 2000)

A study by Kapil et al (2003) identifies the following factors in decreasing order of importance; marketing, entrepreneur's attributes, products, Governmental policies, technology competence, clusters, infrastructure, R&D, company climate, networking and raw material supplies.

Considering the above, in the Goan context, it is very important for the pharmaceutical companies to reorient themselves internally in a way so as to offset the threats if any from the external environment and take advantage of the opportunities emanating from the external environment. The role of the local and national Government as a facilitating and regulating body however cannot be underestimated.

IV. THE MARKET ENVIRONMENT FOR THE PHARMACEUTICAL COMPANIES

The pharmaceutical units in the State depend on the national market for its operating success and growth. Small manufacturing units market their products within the State or nearby states only. Their growth prospects remain restricted to the smallness of the market in which they operate. As selling costs constitute a sizeable chunk of the operating expenses, it is necessary that sales volume increases in proportion to the amount spent on promotion. This is feasible only when large geographical area is covered with which a unit can expect to get a larger share of the market and build up its turnover on a wider base.

Market dynamics have changed in the last few years in India, making the market environment more unstable and complex. Increasing generic penetration, intense competition, fragmentation of the industry has negatively impacted overall value growth of the domestic market. In this scenario, to grow in the domestic market, companies are looking at introducing value added new products, innovation, product life cycle management and increasing their market reach. As the growth opportunities in the domestic market are on a decline, the bigger of the companies are focusing on exports for higher growth and improved margins. However, they face fierce competition from foreign manufacturers with long records of technological growth.

Marketing the pharmaceutical products in countries like UK and USA is not easy even for large Indian companies. It requires a lot of investments and expertise to market the products in these countries. Indian companies are found to be entering into strategic tie- ups with companies in these countries to market their products. Indian companies are required to have WHO certification for their R&D facilities inorder to enter developed countries' markets. It appears that products manufactured in state of the art manufacturing facilities in India and the marketing expertise of the domestic companies will be the key factors in the success of these companies. The market share of even the large–sized pharmaceutical companies is small and they face considerable pressures and uncertainties in sales volume and profitability margins. It can be inferred that only firms with huge financial and infrastructural resources will be able to take advantage of the opportunities thrown open by the new patents regime. At the same time, localized and niche market opportunities will continue to exist which can be exploited by market-focused companies. Exporting into developing country markets is another opportunity for the companies. Entering into marketing and technological collaborations and joint ventures can also give large national companies the competitive edge.

The liberalization of policy regime with respect to the pharmaceutical sector in the 1990s poses many challenges for the small enterprises. With the progressive reduction of list of drugs under the Drug Price Control Order (DPCO), the relaxation granted to the small scale sector's products has been effectively reduced overtime. Finally the small scale units are no more granted exemption even from the diluted DPCO under the new policy regime, reversing the provision granted to the sector since DPCO 1987. The permission of 100 per cent foreign direct investment (FDI) and removal of the restriction on large-size firms required that small firms have to enlarge their market focus and competitive strategies. The adoption of product patent regime and emphasis on quality and good manufacturing practices are likely to demand higher technological efforts from small firms (Lalitha 2004). As small firms are often constrained by their size, limitation in sales, investment, or employment, and small financial resources, meeting these new challenges may not   be as smooth as in the case of large enterprises.

V. SWOT ANALYSIS OF THE PHARMACEUTICAL COMPANIES REGISTERED IN GOA.

Table 1 presents a picture of the size of the pharmaceutical industry in the State of Goa.

Table 1

Composition of the Pharmaceutical Industry in Goa (2005)

No. of Units	50
Large& medium scale industries (Classified by sales turnover - medium, between Rs. 5.0 – 50.0 Cr. & large > Rs. 50.0 Cr.)	74 %
Small scale industries (%) (turnover < 5.0 Cr. Rs.)	26%
Investment in Plant & M/c Rs. (Cr.) 350 Turnover Rs. (Cr.)	2000
Annual growth	18-20 %
Ave. Turnover/unit Rs. (Cr.)	40
Exports Rs. (Cr.)	200
Exports on turnover	10 %
Employment (Tech.)	3500
Employment (Non – Tech)	4500

Source: Cluster development programme, Ministry of SSI, Govt. of India.

As per the cluster development programme of the Government, 74 per cent of the units in Goa are large and medium having sales turnover of more than 5 crore. The remaining 26 per cent are small in terms of sales turnover. The annual growth in the pharmaceutical business in the state is between 18-20 per cent.

According to industry sources, the major issues before the pharmaceutical industry in Goa are:-

i)   Strict compliance to Schedule 'M' of the Drugs &
      Cosmetics Act (A statutory requirement for pharma units)

ii)   Adherence to international standards of quality.

iii) Huge investments for establishing in-house R&D and testing facilities.

iv)   Spurious drugs flooding the market.

v)   Lack of waste disposal facilities.

The following is a SWOT (Strength, Weaknesses, Opportunities and Threats) perspective of the Indian pharmaceutical companies in general.

Strengths of the Indian Pharmaceutical Companies

Considering more than one billion population, it is largely an untapped market. Penetration of modern medicine is less than 30 per cent, implying that there is a huge scope for demand in India.

1.   Fast changing lifestyles opens a huge market for lifestyle drugs, which has a very low contribution in the Indian markets.

2.   One of lowest cost producers of drugs in the world. Cost of production is around 40 to 50 per cent of world average.

3.   Excellent chemistry and process reengineering skills helping in developing cost effective processes.

Weaknesses

1. Marred by the price regulation. The NPPA (National Pharma Pricing Authority) sets prices of different drugs leading to lower profitability.

2. Very low entry barriers make it highly fragmented market. There are about 300 large manufacturing units and about 18,000 small units.

3. Price competition reduces the growth in value term.

Opportunities

1. New patent product regime will bring with it new innovative drugs forcing domestic pharma companies to focus more on R&D.

2. Large numbers of drugs going off-patent in Europe and US during 2005 to 2009 offer a big opportunity.

3. Expansion of healthcare industry due to opening up of health insurance sector and the expected growth in per capita income.

4. Being the lowest cost producer combined with FDA approved plants, Indian companies can become a global outsourcing hub for pharmaceutical products.

Threats

1. Apprehensions over the current structure of new patent regime.

2. Threats from other low cost countries like China and Israel exist.

3. Threat to survival of smaller units.

   The SWOT analysis of the pharmaceutical companies in **Goa**, in particular, reveals the following;

Strengths

- Conducive business environment; Goa's successive Industrial Policy documents gives top priority to pharmaceuticals, drugs and bio- tech industries.
- Developed infrastructure - Transport, power, water availability.
- Existence of auxiliary industries, such as the packaging units.

Weaknesses

- High costs of raw materials.
- With large firms/group of Companies/MNCs being in majority, do not require much of assistance, small industries (which are less in number) are left to fend for themselves. No collective approach/ bargaining to redress problems.
- Absence of common testing facility labs, R&D labs within the state
- Weak capital base forbidding small units to invest further fearing poor viability
- Lack of exposure to enter export market.

Opportunities

- Expanding demand, both domestic and overseas
- Scope for expansion and additional units for generic drugs
- Proximity with Mumbai for raw materials, export and testing facilities
- Opportunities of Globalization such as contract research, contract manufacturing for large MNC's.
- Peaceful social climate with communal harmony.

Threats

- Schedule 'M' involves additional cost, threatens viability & commercial feasibility
- Cut- throat competition, both domestic and external.
- Ceiling on product prices.
- Documentation & procedural hurdles in export marketing.
- Flow of unchecked spurious drugs

Main Observations

The pharmaceutical industry in Goa comprises of units characterized by two extreme/contrast interests. Large companies have adequate resources, whereas tiny units are struggling for survival especially in view of mandatory requirements of GMP. Exemption/ deferment of compliance from certain statutory requirements, especially in adopting Schedule 'M' is the assistance demanded by the small pharmaceutical companies.

The big pharmaceutical companies in Goa are found to be pursuing global strategies to exploit the tremendous opportunities in the generics market abroad and to mitigate the domestic market risk due to demand elasticity, pricing regulation and competition policies. Smaller companies pursue survival strategies by undertaking contract manufacturing or contract research for the bigger firms.

VI. MARKETING PROBLEMS OF THE PHARMACEU-TICAL COMPANIES REGISTERED IN GOA

The pharmaceutical industry requires huge capital investments and expensive product promotions. Indigenous industries find it difficult to create market share for themselves. Besides having to cope with slower revenue growth, pharma companies are facing host of internal and external challenges. In view of the above, it will be useful to analyze Governmental policies and regulations and their impact on the pharmaceutical companies in Goa, as well as the resource constraints faced by the units.

i) Impact of Government's Policy. With the objective of providing impetus to the industrialization process in the backward regions, the government has been adopting area-based tax holiday scheme. As a part of this strategy, specified areas in selected states like Goa, Himachal Pradesh, Uttaranchal, Sikkim, Jammu & Kashmir and Gujarat declared a number of tax incentives like ten-year excise holiday and full income-tax waiver for the specific years. Withdrawal of such concessions in Goa has had a negative impact on the progress of the pharmaceutical industry in the state.

According to some industry experts, this policy has discriminated against small pharmaceutical units who are either forced to migrate or close down. Since regional location of small scale sector is important for meeting requirement of health security at local level, forced concentration of these units in a few tax-free zones is considered undesirable.

Since January 2005, the government has introduced the MRP-based excise duty for the pharmaceutical units in the country. As per this policy, government had levied a 40 per cent excise duty on maximum retail price (MRP) of drugs and not on the manufacturing expenses (i.e. on ex-factory price) which was the practice earlier. Under the new excise scheme, most small scale units are likely to cross the excise exemption limit of Rs 1 crore, thus effectively defeating the basic purpose of small scale exemption limit (Express Pharma Pulse 2005). Under the earlier ex-factory price based excise duty structure majority of small units had a turnover of about Rs. 50 lakhs. Now based on MRP that includes marketing and distribution expenses their turnover is likely to reach Rs. 1 crore. As small units are operating at low profit margins and are incurring additional expenses to upgrade their manufacturing facilities to be GMP compliant, this MRP-based excise regime is going to affect them negatively. In this context, the industry demands that the government should increase the SSI exemption limit for excise from existing Rs. 1 crore of turnover to Rs. 2 crore.

Some of the top echelons of the industry in Goa are also of the view that many of the companies are heading for sickness; the reason being that they are not in a position to make sufficient returns to keep themselves healthy. Profitability has been dropping because of the rigid price controls .Further the complaint is that there is hardly any industry left under price control barring the pharmaceutical industry.

Industry analysts also observe that when product prices are unremunerative, and when companies are not able to cover expenses, it results in the proliferation cf sub-standard products. It was also pointed out that in some states, regulatory body i.e. Food and Drug Authority (FDA) ensures strict compliance to quality based on drug laws, while in others there is virtually no control over the manufacturing activities of the companies. This results in very low costs for those companies, and they in turn get maximum Government tender business which is based on price.

Respondents were also of the view that there are increasingly more regulations on the pharmaceutical industry to drive out the small scale pharmaceutical industry, at the behest of multinational companies.

ii) Infrastructural Constraints. Most pharmaceutical companies are concentrated in the industrial estate at Verna. There has been increasing pressure in terms of demand for additional land, both by the existing and new units. Unavailability of land affects the expansion prospects of existing companies.

Erratic power supply and inadequate water at times results in losses in production. Absence of a common testing and R&D laboratory are stated to be the other infrastructural limitations of the state. Industrialists are also concerned about the supply of adequate and quality manpower. The pharmaceutical industry which is a knowledge based industry requires pharmacists and scientists. With Goa College of Pharmacy having limited seats, it is pointed out that there is an acute shortage of chemists that can be employed in the sector.

VII. INDIVIDUAL COMPANY LEVEL ANALYSIS OF MARKETING PROBLEMS

i. Geno Pharmaceuticals Limited

Geno feels that price controls over the industry are too rigid. Excessive government regulations have strong effect on profitability of the company, especially since the price of basic raw materials and the cost of packing have shot up over the past five years. The small size in comparison to the large Indian and Multinational companies acts as an entry barrier to high value therapeutic segments. The company feels that it has a price disadvantage over larger competitors due to lower economies of scale. It does not have required exposure to intellectual property rights issues.

The problems faced by the company in exporting are as follows;

1. Lack of information of export market.
2. Price competition.
3. World Trade Organization regulations
4. Customs duties and formalities

The company ranks the main competitive pressures facing it in the following order;

1. Competitor rivalry.
2. Bargaining by retailers.
3. Threat of substitutes
4. High distribution costs
5. Threat of new entrants.

Geno faces the following marketing problems due to the changed economic environment, characterized by globalization and intensive competition;

1. Competition from Multinational Companies and other large Indian companies.

2. Government policies and procedures.

3. Inadequate technology and resources for R&D

The company seeks export incentives specifically from the State Government as there are only central schemes for exports in general and not those which provides specific impetus to the pharma sector. It also seeks reduction in price controls, and procedural formalities, inorder to improve its market performance and future growth prospects.

ii. Wallace Pharmaceuticals Private Limited

According to Wallace, pharmaceutical manufacturers have suffered from high transaction costs, including obstacles and difficulties associated with administrative processes, dishonesty of public agents, delays in obtaining finance, and transportation bottlenecks. It also faces marketing problems due to excessive staff turnover.

Company sources state that Government control over pricing is adversely affecting its performance in terms of profitability and R & D. The company feels that Government should reduce its span of control and let the market forces take care of price mechanism.

Wallace listed the following as the main problems faced while exporting its products;

1. Lack of information of export markets

2. Price competition.

The existence of a spurious drug market and duplication of products is another area of concern of Wallace Pharmaceuticals.

Copying of the company's products by unethical marketers affects the market prospects of Wallace. To overcome this threat the company is in the process of using holograms in its packaging so that copying or duplicating the product will become difficult.

The company seeks the following measures of assistance from the Government for its marketing success:

1. Stable policies on prices.
2. New drug policy to be implemented at the earliest.
3. Enhancement of limit to be categorized as Small Scale Industry.
4. Incentives for implementing Schedule 'M'.

iii. Kare Pharmaceuticals Private Limited

The company states that its main problems in marketing are inadequate technology and resources to compete with large pharmaceutical companies. It was also expressed that bigger companies have an advantage in marketing of their products.

It was pointed out that there are too many taxes on the sale of medicines. These include customs duty (39.20 percent), excise duty (4 per cent), sales tax (state 6-12 per cent, central- 4 per cent), turnover tax (1-3 per cent), octroi/entry tax (upto 2.5 per cent.). This erodes the competitive advantage of firms with fewer resources.

Price competition is considered at Kare as the main problem adversely affecting its exports. The company's chosen market segments are clogged with intense competition and the main competitive pressures facing the company, listed in order of severity are ;-

1. Threat of substitutes.
2. Bargaining of buyers.
3. Bargaining of distributors.

4.   Competitor rivalry.

5.   Threat of new entrants.

The company seeks total decontrol on prices to improve its performance and to achieve a turnaround in business. It has been continuously incurring losses over the recent years. The main demand is to do away with the maximum retail price-based excise collection, which resulted in 6,000 formulation units losing more than half of their business to larger companies, which set up manufacturing units in excise-free zones. The company also seeks total eradication of the spurious drugs industry which affects the prospects of genuine players. Another main demand of the company is that the Government should provide long term loans with low rate of interest to enable pharma companies to set up R&D labs, and low rates of import duties on equipment imported for R&D.

iv. Cosme Farma Laboratories Limited

Relating to Government's pricing policy, the management at CFL is of the view that price control and product regulation should be there only for those molecules and therapy that are used to control epidemics. It was also expressed that there should be effective control on OTC medicines (Over- The –Counter) and their advertising.

It faces threats due to spurious, sub-standard substitutes that find their way in the market.The main problems in marketing that are faced by the company are:

1.   Less capital for R&D and hence difficulties in accessing developed countries markets.

2.   High freight and raw materials cost.

3.   Distributional and logistics problems.

4.   Competition from large companies.

CFL would like the Government to implement an uniform excise duty and policy as well as reduction in excise duty. Assistance for infrastructural development such as better roads, power and water supply would increase efficiencies and help in better market performance of the company.

v. Toyo Laboratories Private Limited

Excessive competition in local markets, unethical practices adopted by competitors, and doctor-chemist-manufacturer nexus in rural markets are stated by Toyo as the main pressures faced while marketing of its products. The company feels it does not have competitive strength in accessing foreign markets and in technology. It does not use IT related systems and processes in promotion and distribution.

Lack of knowledge of export markets and inadequate capital for investment are listed by Toyo as the main marketing constraints faced. It is felt that bigger companies have strong marketing and distribution capabilities which provide them with a competitive edge.

The company faces the following obstacles in marketing:

1. Price competition.
2. Threat of substitutes.
3. Inefficient delivery services.
4. Unethical practices adopted by competitors.

Toyo states that prices of products are controlled by brand leader, and that small firms like it have to keep prices almost 10 to 15 per cent lower than the brand leader. This squeezes profitability of the firm. National Pharmaceutical Pricing Authority's price fixation policy, according to the firm, does not allow small units to compete with brands already established in the market.

The company had to retrench from unprofitable markets and reduce the number of products offered in the market, in the face of increasing competition in the recent years.

vi. Merit Pharmaceuticals Private Limited

Merit considers price regulations on the small pharmaceutical industry as too unrealistic, as it does not take into account marketing costs and margin of the small manufacturers.

The main problems in marketing as expressed by the company are;

1. Financial constraints and inability to access timely finance.
2. Inability to access foreign markets.
3. Difficulty in getting qualified and trained marketing personnel.
4. Unethical marketing practices adopted by big companies even in rural markets, which are the targets of the small firms.
5. High costs of raw materials.

The company seeks protectionist measures from the Government, in the form of tax concessions, reduction of excise duties, price preference policy in Government purchase programme etc. to enable small companies to survive the competition.

vii. Goa Anti-biotics and Pharmaceuticals Limited (GAPL)

It was disclosed that the company was not getting enough government attention as required and neither was it receiving any medicine orders in bulk. Company sources also stated that though the medicines manufactured by GAPL were reasonably less than other manufacturers it was necessary that the government makes it compulsory for the GMC, health centres, ESI hospitals to purchase medicines from the GAPL, as this would help it to cover costs.

Sources also revealed that GAPL's products did not command the required trust of private doctors, and that the company is purely dependent on orders from Government. If particular orders are below a certain minimum required batch size, it is uneconomical to produce, thus resulting in losses. GAPL has stopped promotion through medical representatives inorder to cut costs.

Among the two main decisions taken by the current directors is that the excess staff that was not required should be removed so that the expenditure could be curtailed, besides this a recommendation has been made to the Economic Development Corporation with regards to voluntary retirement of some of the employees.

The Company was registered with BIFR as a sick company in 1997. Frequent management changes, administrative hurdles, bureaucratic interference and lack of a market oriented vision are stated as major hurdles affecting company performance.

VIII. MAIN FINDINGS AND OBSERVATIONS

An analysis of the marketing problems of the individual companies indicates that fragmentation of the industry causes pressures on profitability of the bigger companies in the group and threatens the survival of the small companies. In such a scenario, Government price and product policy also discriminates against the small companies, enabling large multinationals to manipulate markets, distributors, and doctors.

Majority of the companies, big as well as small, expressed resentment over the rigid price controls which adversely affected the profitability of the companies. As big multinationals can compete on the basis of higher volumes and coverage of bigger geographic areas, they follow a strategy of offsetting the advantageous position of local companies by setting lower prices in export markets. This acts as a major constraint in exporting for local firms.

Respondent companies also expressed fear about the unethical promotional standards adopted by big competitors, which affects the market of the genuine players. Besides this high costs and lack of supportive measures and incentives from the Government are viewed as negative factors affecting the marketing of pharmaceutical products by local manufacturers.

Based on individual company level analysis, the main problems affecting companies are grouped as in Table 2.

Table 2

Marketing Problems affecting the Pharmaceutical Industry in Goa

Nature of Problem	Problem due to	No of firms Affected	Mean score	% of firms
Group I Size	• Small size • Lower economies of scale	2 2	2	28.5
Group II Infrastructure &location	• Inadequate infrastructure(land, water, power, road) • Locational disadvantages	2 2	2	28.5
GROUP III Pricing & terms of selling	• Rigid price control • Price competition • Difficulty in managing distribution channels • High prices of raw materials	4 4 3 3	3.5	50

GROUP IV
Marketing &
sales promo.
	• Inability to access foreign markets
	• Inadequate market intelligence
	• WTO formalities/ IPR issues
	• Lack of marketing assistance
	• Inability to use IT related systems
	  and processes in marketing
	• Lack of sales force management
	  and control
		2
		3
		3
		1
		2
		
		3
			2.3	32.8

Group V Impact of present disturbances	• Impact of globalisation • Entry of MNCS • Spurious drug market/unethical promotion • Lack of supportive Govt. measures	3 4 6 4	4.25	60.7
Group VI Facilitating functions and services	• Inadequate financial resources • Less capital for R&D • High import duties • Administrative delays and hurdles • Inadequate packaging • Absence of common R&D/ testing lab.	2 3 2 1 1 1	1.8	25.7

Source: *Primary data*

The mean score in the table refers to the average number of firms afflicted due to problems in each of the categories as shown in the table.

The various problems afflicting the pharmaceutical companies in Goa, in varying degrees can be summed up as follows.

i)   Lack of training and finance for technological up-gradation to meet global quality standards especially of the very small companies in the selected group.

ii)   Rigid price controls

iii) Price competition

iv)   Difficulties in managing distribution channels

v)   Limited exposure and expertise on Intellectual Property Rights issues.

vi)   Limited adoption of information technology (IT) techniques in marketing.

vii) Low R&D expenditure of the medium companies and negligible R&D expenditure of the smaller companies, which affects the ability of these companies to offer innovative solutions.

viii) The inability of the smaller companies in the selected group to access finance on easy terms for import of capital goods and to undertake advertising and marketing activities.

ix) Spurious drug market and unethical promotion.

x) Lack of supportive measures from the Government

xi) High prices of raw materials.

It is clear from the table that 60.7 per cent of the companies feel the heat of competitive market environment and lack of support and incentives from the Government. Fifty per cent of the firms are adversely affected by price policy and the terms of selling. Problems directly related to marketing such as inability to access export markets, lack of clarity on WTO/IPR related issues, and lack of sales force management and control afflict 32.8 per cent of the firms. Firms are also at a disadvantage due to their small size in relation to global majors, and due to infrastructural bottlenecks.

IX.   IMPLICATIONS AND SUGGESTIONS

The main implications related to the above findings are as follows;

1.   The product patent regime will make it obligatory for Indian companies to compete in R&D if they want to survive. Similarly, WTO led global trading system will result in import tariffs coming down. For Indian companies to compete with cheap imports, they will have to invest in cost effective technology and processes. Therefore, it is imperative that the pharma industry has surplus for investment. In this context, a liberalized price control regime becomes more important.

2. It is observed that the sector is seriously concerned about the problem of spurious drugs, which has to be tackled by state FDA by proper regulation and control of manufacturing processes, materials used, labeling and packaging.

3. The need is expressed for accredited testing laboratories that are well equipped and adequately staffed. The staff should be trained well for drawing samples for test and monitoring the quality of drugs and cosmetics moving in the State.

4. It is observed that majority of the companies do not have enough resources for R&D investment. The companies under study could exploit its know-how in herbal medicines. Since these medicines do not come under the purview of the TRIPS regime and the research in new chemical entities involves millions of dollars of investment, the companies should engage in R&D in herbal medicine. The companies could try to exploit the Indian traditional knowledge in ayurveda and herbal cures.

5. The bigger of the companies should not wait for doles and incentives from the Government but should focus on increasing their market reach and developing their core competencies.

X. CONCLUSION

The study of the marketing problems of individual companies leads to the conclusion, that cut-throat competition, inadequacy of financial and technological resources and lack of support from the Government threatens the sustainability, in particular, of the small firms. The pharmaceutical companies in Goa, irrespective of size, feel the adverse impact of globalization, entry of MNCs and lack of supportive measures from the Government. Unfair price competition by pharma majors who compete on higher volumes and lower costs adds to the woes of local companies. Hence, it is imperative that the pharmaceutical companies in

Goa lower costs, by aiming at better production and marketing efficiencies.

The smaller firms are constrained in their marketing efforts by the lack of resources and need to be brought under the cluster development programme by the Government to provide them comprehensive support.

The study also arrives at the conclusion that there is an urgent need to set up accredited testing laboratories in the state that are well equipped and adequately staffed. The staff should be trained well for drawing samples for test and monitoring the quality of drugs and cosmetics moving in the State.

It is imperative that the local as well as the central Governments puts systems, procedures and regulations in place that will help monitor the type of drugs produced and sold in the country, as well as to determine the unethical promotion resorted to by some companies, so that the prospects of genuine players are not adversely affected.

References

Confederation of Indian Industries (2004), 'Sector Report on Drugs and Pharmaceuticals,' http://ciionline.org/busserv/drugs/

Company Annual Reports, 2002-07, Registrar of Companies, Goa

Express Pharma Pulse, Various Issues, Mumbai.

Endersby, J.M, "Kick Starting Bio-technology in Ontario," *Nature Biotechnology* 17 (1999), 444-445

Giesecke, S (2000), "The Contrasting Roles of Government in the Development of the Biotechnology Industry in the US and Germany," Research Policy, 29, pp. 205-233.

Goa Survey (2009), 'Pharma on a Healthy Growth Curve,' *Business India,* February 22, 2009.

Government of India, (2005), *'Cluster Development Programme (CDP) of Ministry of SSI,'* http://sisigoa.nic.in/clusterdevprog.htm

Gupta, Ashok; Raj, S. P; Wileman D (1986), "A Model for studying R& D – Marketing interface in the Product Growth Process," *Journal of Marketing,* 50, 7-17.

Hamel, Gary; Prahalad, C. K. (1994), 'Competing for the Future,' *Harvard Business Review,* July-Aug 1994, pp. 123.

ICRA (1999) *'Industry Watch Series:* The Indian Pharmaceutical Industry.'

Jayakrishna, S (2006), "New Age Pharma Marketing," *Marketing Mastermind, the ICFAI University,* Press, Hyderabad, pp 37-43.

Kapil, N. K; Nagar, K. N; Kapil, S (2003), "Critical Success Factors for Small Scale Pharmaceutical Companies," *NMIS Management Review,* Vol XV No. 2, pp 11-39

Lalitha, N(2001), *"Product Patents and the Pharmaceutical Industry, "* A Report submitted to the Indian Council of Social Science research, New Delhi.

___(2002), "Indian Drug Industry in the WTO Regime," *Economic and Political Weekly,* Vol. XXXVII, No. 34, 3542-3555.

Nair, M.D. (2002), "An Industry in Transition: The Indian Pharmaceutical Industry," *Journal of Intellectual Property Rights,* 7(5), pp 405-415

Pradhan, J. P. (2007), "New Policy Regime and Small Pharmaceutical Firms in India," Working Paper, 2007/02, Institute for Studies in Industrial Development

Unnikrishna, Rajesh (2005), "Global Generic Drug Companies Descend on India," *The Financial Express,* March 14, 2005

5

"A CRITICAL EVALUATION OF ICDS (INTEGRATED CHILD DEVELOPMENT SERVICES) PROGRAMME IN GOA"

— *Agnela A.D. Dias**

INTRODUCTION

The ICDS Scheme was launched by the Department of Social Welfare, Government of India, in pursuance of the National Policy for Children. The ICDS Programme seeks to lay a solid foundation for the development of the nation's human resources by providing an integrated package of childhood services. The National Policy for children (1974) recognizes the supreme importance of children's programmes in the development of human resources that are vital to social and economic progress. The Directorate of Women and Child Development in Goa is carrying out the work of ICDS Programme through its Director, Deputy Director, Social Welfare Officers (SWO), Programme Officer (PO), Child Development Project Officers (CDPOs), Supervisors (Mukhya Sevikas), Anganwadi workers and helpers at the anganwadi centres. An anganwadi worker heads one group of ICDS (Integrated Child Development Services) Programme beneficiaries or one anganwadi. The ICDS Programme functions in all the talukas of Goa and its services were extended to the

**Associate Professor and Head, Department of Economics, Government College of Arts, Science and Commerce, Sanquelim- Goa.*

rural areas of Goa.The Central and State Government, funds the ICDS Programme in Goa, but all the benefits do not reach the beneficiaries. Political pressures, inefficient management, malpractices etc have come to light in Goa, which affected the implementation of ICDS (Integrated Child Development Services) Programme in Goa.

This paper highlights the shortcomings in the working of ICDS (Integrated Child Development Services) Programme in Goa. Section I covers an introduction. Section II covers the scope and relevance of the study, whereas the objectives of the study are included under section III of my study. Sections IV and V covers the methodology of the study and the limitations. A detailed explanation of the critical evaluation of ICDS Programme in Goa is included under section VI. The findings, conclusions and the recommendations are covered under section VII, section VIII and section IX of my study.

The broad objectives of the ICDS (Integrated Child Development Services) Programme is improvement in the nutritional and health status of children in the age group of 0-6 years, reduction in incidence of mortality, morbidity, malnutrition and school dropouts and enhancing the capabilities of mothers to take care of the nutritional needs of the child. Special attention was to be given to the malnourished children of grade III and grade IV and "at risk" mothers.The Government of India introduced the ICDS (Integrated Child Development Services) since 1976, as a maternal and Child Welfare Programme.

SCOPE AND RELEVANCE OF THE STUDY

The study covers the entire state of Goa. The relevance of this study becomes obvious, if one considers the ever-increasing role and importance of children in the emerging socio-economic scenario of the country. There is extensive awakening in present day Indian society, to the problems of children. Therefore, any scheme meant for the amelioration of the socio-economic conditions of children needs to be thoroughly studied, to assess their efficacy in reaching out the targets.

Till date, no such studies have been carried out on the operation of the scheme in Goa. This research critically evaluates the functioning of ICDS (Integrated Child Development Services) Programme in Goa. Based on the findings, suggestions and recommendations are made for the improvement of the functioning of the ICDS Programme.

This study will also help the policy makers and the Government to rectify their policy, with regards to the development of children in Goa.It will also help the Government of Goa to take corrective steps and bring about changes wherever needed. A detailed study of this scheme will perhaps help the central Government to make decisions in the future with regards to launching of similar schemes\Programmes.

OBJECTIVES OF THE STUDY

The following are the aims and objectives of the study.

1.   To examine the socio-economic background of the beneficiaries of ICDS Programme in Goa.

2.   To examine the problems faced by the beneficiaries of ICDS Programme in Goa.

3.   To examine the implementation of ICDS Programme in Goa.

4.   To identify the problems faced by the implementing agency of ICDS Programme in Goa.

5.   To analyse the achievements and shortcomings of ICDS Programme in Goa.

6.   To draw appropriate conclusions and make relevant recommendations\suggestions.

METHODOLOGY OF THE STUDY

The data for this study was collected from both primary and secondary sources.

The primary data was collected through interview schedules, interviews and observations.

In Goa under the ICDS scheme there were a total number of 1004 anganwadis when the research was carried out of which a sample of 5% had been considered under this study. This 5% of the anganwadis amounted to 51 anganwadis of Goa of which, 25 anganwadis from North Goa and 26 anganwadis from South Goa had been considered. This study covered 50% of the child beneficiaries of each of the 51 anganwadis of Goa. A total of 429 parents of the beneficiaries (children) attending the anganwadis had been interviewed which included 217 parents from North Goa and 212 parents from South Goa.

The primary data was collected through interview schedules, from the parents of the beneficiaries of the anganwadis under the ICDS programme. Interviews were held with the Child Development Programme Officers, Mukhya Sevikas, the Director of the Directorate of Women and Child Development, Panaji Goa, Block Development Officers and the Deputy Director of Rural Development Agency Panaji Goa.

"Convenient sampling" was used under the sampling design inorder to collect information from the parents of the beneficiaries of ICDS Programme, anganwadi workers and also the BDOs. The CDPOs associated with the ICDS Programme were interviewed. Primary data was also collected through observations of the anganwadis.

The secondary data was collected from journals, books, official records of the Directorate of women and child Development, Panaji, the official records of the Child Development Project offices of Goa and the official records of the Rural Development

Agency office of Goa. The statistical tools used in the analysis are (1) Mean and (2) Percentage.

LIMITATIONS OF THE STUDY

Some of the past official records with reference to the ICDS Programme of Goa were not available. Some of the ICDS authorities were not ready to furnish some of the details of the working of the Programme at the taluka level.

From the target group of the ICDS Programme in Goa only the information of the children beneficiaries attending the anganwadis was collected.

CRITICAL EVALUATION OF ICDS PROGRAMME IN GOA

The evaluation of ICDS Programme in Goa includes an introduction on ICDS in Goa, socio-economic profile of ICDS Programme beneficiaries of Goa, the criteria for determining the success of ICDS Programme in Goa, various other aspects about ICDS Programme in Goa and the monitoring authority of ICDS Programme in Goa.

(I) Introduction on ICDS in Goa.

Initially the ICDS Programme in Goa was solely financed by the central government but now the ICDS Programme in Goa is partly financed by the state government.

Taluka-wise total number of anganwadis and the year of commencement of ICDS programme in different talukas of Goa.

The following table shows the taluka-wise details of total number of anganwadis and the year of commencement of ICDS Programme under different talukas of Goa.

Table No 1

Table Showing Taluka-wise Total Number of Anganwadis and the Year of Commencement of ICDS Programme in Different Talukas of Goa.

TALUKAS	YEAR OF COMMENCEMENT OF ICDS PROGRAMME	TOTAL NUMBER OF ANGANWADIS UNDER ICDS
Bicholim	1978	87
Pernem	1978-79	63
Sanguem	1980	60
Sattari	1981-82	82
Quepem	1982-83	66
Canacona	1982	44
Ponda	1983	119
Bardez	1983-84	132
Salcete	, 1986	170
Tiswadi	1986	90
Mormugao	1988-89	91

Source: *ICDS Offices at the taluka level.*

From the table it is clear that the ICDS Programme commenced in Goa in Bicholim taluka in1987. When the research was carried out a total of 1004 anganwadis existed under the ICDS Scheme in Goa. As per the Economic Survey (2010-11) done by the Directorate of Planning, Statistics and Evaluation, Government of Goa, the number of anganwadis have increased to 1262. Under the Supplementary Nutrition Programme of ICDS Scheme, 59619 beneficiaries (Children between 6 months to 6 years and pregnant and lactating mothers) are being provided dry as well as cooked diet enriched with nutrition and protein. An anganwadi is allocated for a population of 1,000 people and a minimum of 25 children can be enrolled under an anganwadi. A panel consisting of a CDPO, Programme Officer, doctor from a health centre and the BDO (Block Development Officer) selects an anganwadi worker. An anganwadi worker is normally required to work from 8 a.m. to 12.45 noon.

(1) The Socio-Economic Profile of the ICDS Programme Beneficiaries of Goa.

The socio-economic profile of the ICDS Programme beneficiaries of Goa encompasses the following.

(a) Age-group of the ICDS beneficiaries, annual family income of the beneficiaries, caste and religion.

(b) Educational qualification of parents.

The socio-economic profile of the ICDS Programme beneficiaries in Goa helps us to know the economic and social status of the beneficiaries. The socio-economic profile of the ICDS beneficiaries of Goa also helped in arriving at various conclusions. A total of 429 parents of the beneficiaries (children) of ICDS registered under the anganwadis of Goa were interviewed which included 217 parents of the ICDS beneficiaries from North Goa and 212 parents of the ICDS beneficiaries from South Goa.

(a) Age-group of the ICDS beneficiaries, annual family income of the beneficiaries, caste and religion.

It was seen from the statistics gathered through field work that all the beneficiaries of ICDS Programme attending the anganwadis were within the prescribed age limit. It showed that precautions were taken in Goa to see that the children from the wrong age group did not take the benefits of ICDS Programme. The majority of the ICDS Programme beneficiaries belonged to the age-group of 4 to 5 years. No beneficiaries belonged to the age-group of 0-1 year probably because they were infants and needed a lot of care from the mothers.

It showed that majority of the ICDS Programme beneficiaries had an annual family income of less than Rs. 5,000. It also showed that majority of the families of the ICDS beneficiaries attending the anganwadis were living below the poverty line. It was concluded from this that the benefits of the ICDS Programme in Goa were going to very poor people of Goa coming from a poor economic background.

It was also seen that the majority i.e. 56.67% of the ICDS Programme beneficiaries in Goa belonged to the general category which included 53.53% beneficiaries from North Goa and 16.08% beneficiaries from South Goa. Around 3.03% of the ICDS beneficiaries attending the anganwadis in Goa were SC and 1.16% were ST. The beneficiaries belonging to the general category also took advantage of this programme in Goa. Around 5.36% of the beneficiaries belonging to the other backward category were from North Goa and 30.76% were from South Goa.

We could infer that not only the SC, ST and OBC benefits from the ICDS scheme in Goa, but majority of the beneficiaries attending the anganwadis were from the general category i.e. 59.67%. The ICDS Programme in Goa catered to all castes and categories in Goa.

It was found that majority i.e. 92.07% of the ICDS beneficiaries in Goa were hindus whereas 6.99% were muslims and 0.93% were Christians. It showed that people of all religions had taken the benefit of this Programme in Goa. Majority of the beneficiaries attending the anganwadis were hindus, this was probably because the hindu population is more in Goa.

(b) Educational qualification of the parents of the ICDS beneficiaries of Goa

The educational qualification of the father and mother also affected the children as ICDS beneficiaries. From the field survey it was found that 15.15% of the mothers of the beneficiaries of ICDS Programme were having a qualification of SSC, but 27.27% of their mothers were illiterate. It was also seen that 3.03% of the mothers of the ICDS beneficiaries had done some courses, 24%

had studied upto the primary level and 30.30% had high school education. Only one of the beneficiaries had lost the mother. We concluded that majority of the mothers of the ICDS programme beneficiaries were not highly qualified and some of them were illiterate.

In addition to this, 39.86% of the fathers of the beneficiaries were educated upto high school and 19.11% were educated upto the primary school. It is also seen that 6.75% of the fathers of the ICDS beneficiaries had done some courses and 17.71% of the fathers of the ICDS beneficiaries had completed SSC, while 15.85% of the fathers of the ICDS beneficiaries were illiterate. It was also seen that three beneficiaries had lost their father.

Majority of the parents of the anganwadi beneficiaries attending the anganwadis were either illiterate or had primary level education or high school education. This shows that the ICDS Programme beneficiaries do not come from highly qualified family backgrounds. This low family educational background added to the family's ignorance, lack of knowledge, carelessness etc.

(2) The criteria for determining the success of ICDS programme in Goa.

Under the criteria for determining the success of ICDS Programme in Goa two aspects were taken into consideration, which are as follows.

(a)   Health and

(b)   Nutrition\ food served

Malnutrition could not be taken as criteria as the data was not available. Therefore only two criterias were considered.

(a) Health

Inorder to get a better picture of ICDS Programme functioning and its success the responses were presented in the form of tables showing the health of children before joining the ICDS Programme as well as after joining the ICDS Programme. Besides this, the type of food supposed to be served by the anganwadis and the actual food served was shown. The calorie intake of the food served to the ICDS Programme beneficiaries actually attending the anganwadis was calculated. Whether the food served was according to the timetable or not was also found out.

It was observed that before joining the ICDS, 81.81% of the beneficiaries were taken to the doctor annually only 1 to 5 times, whereas 17.01% of the ICDS beneficiaries were taken to the doctor around 5 to 10 times, and 1.16% of the ICDS beneficiaries were taken to the doctor more than 10 times annually. But after joining the anganwadis, 68.53% of the beneficiaries were taken to the doctor annually for 1 to 5 times. It is also seen that 30.30% of the beneficiaries visited the doctor 5 to 10 times after joining the ICDS. This increase in the number of beneficiaries from 17.01% to 30.30% could be because of poor nutrition, lack of hygiene at the anganwadis, improper infrastructure at the anganwadis, no proper storehouses for the foodgrains, leaking roofs during the rains, insects, rats, no proper kitchens, flies, no proper floors (potholes in the floor), mud floors, no toilets, no proper water supply facilities, no proper and timely medical checkups, no proper airy rooms, etc which added to the ill health of the ICDS beneficiaries actually attending the anganwadis. It was also observed that 1.16% of the children under the anganwadis were taken to the doctor 10-15 times before joining the anganwadis, but after joining the anganwadis the number had remained the same.

(b) Nutrition\ Food served

Balanced nutrition for pre-school children of 0- 5 years should be part of an overall strategy of preventive healthcare of which the main components would be adequate nutritious foods, environmental sanitation and immunization.

2.1 Food supposed to be served during the week by the Anganwadis of Goa and the calorie intake by the beneficiaries

From the field survey it was seen that the anganwadis under the ICDS Programme in Goa had been provided with a timetable of food to be served to the children attending the anganwadis. After finding about the food supplied to each child under the anganwadis the calorie intake of the food eaten by the children per day was calculated with the help of a dietician from Goa Medical College. Supplementary support for the calorie calculation had been taken from the books from Goa Medical College.

According to the dietician at Goa Medical College the children under the anganwadis should be provided with a calorie intake of 250 calories per day through supplementary nutrition as these children come from poor families, but it had been seen that these children did not get adequate calories every day. This was likely to affect the physical as well as the mental growth of children. In Goa under the ICDS Scheme it was seen that the calorie intake of the children of the anganwadis on four days of a week was far less than the normal requirement of 250 calories per day. This was the root cause of malnutrition of various grades in Goa

Initially the government used to provide 95 paise per child per day for food intake under the anganwadis, but after August 2002 with additional central assistance of 55 paise the total amount of money provided to each child for food intake was Rs. 1.50 paise per day. Initially the malnourished children were provided with Rs. 1.35 paise per day, but with additional central assistance of 55 paise the total amount of food provided to these malnourished children was of Rs. 1.90 paise per day. The amount of money allocated for each child for food\nutrition under the ICDS scheme i.e. for the normal children as well as the children belonging to various grades of malnutrition was too less.

2.2 Food served according\ not according to the timetable, to the ICDS beneficiaries of Goa.

Some of the anganwadis of Goa under the ICDS Programme did not serve food according to the timetable.It was seen that 50.34% of the beneficiaries were not supplied food according to the timetable. This showed the carelessness of the anganwadi workers. This had resulted in increase in the number of children with different grades of malnutrition. Infact a proper monitoring of the work by the authorities could have helped in overcoming this shortcoming in the working of ICDS in Goa. This negligence on the part of the anganwadi workers had affected the future labour force of our state. It had also aggravated the problem of malnourishment in Goa.

(3) Various other aspects about ICDS programme of Goa.

This section encompasses the following sub-sections.

(i)   Other details of ICDS Programme in Goa.

(ii) Total number of surveyed anganwadis, total number of children belonging to below poverty line and the total number of children in the anganwadis absent on the day of the field visit.

(iii) Non-availability of basic amenities in the anganwadis of Goa.

(iv) Problems\malpractices under the anganwadis, according to the parents of the beneficiaries.

(i) Other details of ICDS

The other details of the ICDS Programme covered are shown below.

(a)   Whether the child longs to go to the anganwadis or not.

(b)   Proper care taken\not taken of the children by the anganwadi workers.

(c) Whether the anganwadi workers and helpers carry out their work and responsibilities efficiently or not.

(d) Whether the anganwadi workers feed the children properly or not.

(e) Whether proper pre-school education is imparted\not imparted.

(f) Whether the anganwadi workers and helpers follow strict working hours or not.

(g) Annual Absenteeism of the anganwadi workers.

It was found that 32.16% of the parents of the beneficiaries of ICDS Programme said that their children did not long to go to the anganwadis. This probably could be because the children at the anganwadis did not like the environment, lack of toys at the anganwadis, tasteless food served at the anganwadis,etc.

It was seen that 11.18% of the parents of the beneficiaries felt that the anganwadi workers did not take proper care of the children which included 0.46% from North Goa and 10.72% from South Goa. This could be because of lack of proper knowledge about childcare, ignorance, inefficiency in work, lack of accountability, etc.

About 30.76% of the parents of the beneficiaries felt that the anganwadi workers and helpers did not carry out their work and responsibilities properly. This was probably because they were not duty conscious; there may be no proper monitoring by the higher authorities, no accountability of work carried out, carelessness, etc.

It was also observed from the table that 80.65% of the parents of the beneficiaries felt that no proper care was taken by the anganwadi workers to feed the children. This probably may be due to inefficiency in work, lack of training, no proper knowledge about nutritional needs of children, no proper checks by the authorities, etc.

It was observed that 64.56% of the parents of the beneficiaries felt that proper non-formal pre-school teaching was not imparted to the children. This was probably because the anganwadi workers were not made accountable in imparting proper informal education. Besides, creative thinking was not encouraged. There were no proper books, no educative toys, no educative posters, no drawing colours, etc. at some of the anganwadi centres.

It was also seen that 41.49% of the anganwadi workers and helpers did not follow strict working hours. This showed the carelessness of the workers towards their duties. Besides this, about 25.49% of the anganwadi workers were absent between10-20 days at the anganwadis annually. It was also seen that 11.76% of the anganwadi workers were absent between 20 to 30 days annually at the anganwadis and 39.21 % of the anganwadi workers were absent for 30 to 40 days annually at the anganwadis.Whatever be the reason for absence, a substitute anganwadi worker should be provided inorder to carry out the work in her absence, so as not to affect the functioning of the anganwadis.

(II) Total number of Surveyed Anganwadis, total number of children belonging to below poverty line list and the total number of children in the Anganwadis absent on the day of the field visit.

The field survey covered 25 anganwadis of North Goa and 26 anganwadis of South Goa. A total of 429 children were surveyed under this study, out of which a total of 68 children from North Goa and 164 children from South Goa belonged to the BPL list. The children belonging to families above the poverty line were also taking advantage of the ICDS Scheme in Goa.It was also seen that many children were absent at the anganwadis on the day of the field visit to the anganwadis.This showed that all was not well with the functioning of the scheme in Goa.

(III) Non-availability of basic amenities in the Anganwadis of Goa.

Out of the 51 anganwadis surveyed under this study which included 25 anganwadis from North Goa and 26 anganwadis from South Goa showed that 47.05% of the anganwadis in Goa did not have play grounds, 76.47% of the anganwadis did not have electricity supply, and 66.66% did not have water supply connections in the anganwadis and 50. 98% of the anganwadis did not have toilets. It was also seen that 45.09% of the anganwadis did not have airy rooms and no proper windows for the anganwadis. In Goa 29.41% of the anganwadis did not have proper chairs and tables for the beneficiaries. Around 23.52% of the anganwadis did not have toys and 33.33% of the anganwadis did not have different types of books for the beneficiaries. All this showed the inadequacy of basic amenities and infrastructure in some of the anganwadis of Goa, which reflected the poor support received from the related services. Health education may be there but absence of basic amenities hinders, hygiene and sanitation.

(IV) Problems\ malpractices under Anganwadis according to the parents of the beneficiaries.

It was seen from the study that 2.33% of the parents complained that the selection of anganwadi workers was done through pressure and 2.33% of the parents expressed that the anganwadi workers pocketed foodstuff from the anganwadis. Besides this, according to 34.03% of the parents of the beneficiaries, the anganwadi workers did not abide by the time schedule of work, 22.84% parents of the ICDS beneficiaries complained about improper infrastructure at the anganwadis, 14.91% complained about unhygienic anganwadis and 7.22% complained about congested rooms of the anganwadis. It was also seen that 4.66% of the parents of the beneficiaries complained that there was no provision of toys and books, 22.61% of the parents of the beneficiaries complained about the mud floors of the anganwadis and 1.39% of the parents of the beneficiaries complained about leaking roofs of the anganwadis during the rains. According to 2.33% of the parents of the beneficiaries, the anganwadis did not maintain proper records and according to 3.96% of the parents of the beneficiaries, the anganwadis did not have proper doors. All these shortcomings under the anganwadis, affected the functioning of ICDS in Goa. We can conclude that according to the parents of the children attending the anganwadis the infrastructural problems were many. This was accompanied by problems of inefficiencies by the anganwadi workers and political pressures which affected the selection of the anganwadi workers. Selection of anganwadi workers through pressure led to selection of anganwadi workers who were not competent enough to carry out the work of managing the anganwadi.

V. The Monitoring Authority of ICDS programme in Goa

There existed some limitations in the working of the monitoring authority of ICDS Scheme in Goa. Under the ICDS Scheme in Goa the monitoring authority at the apex consists of the Director of the Directorate of Women and Child Development, under whom the various Child Development Project Officers (CDPOs) at the taluka level function. The Mukhya Sevikas (Supervisors) function under the eleven CDPOs of Goa at the taluka level. The anganwadi workers of ICDS Programme under different talukas work under the supervision of the Mukhya Sevikas of Goa. If only this hierarchy of personnel had taken up their responsibilities seriously, the working and implementation of the ICDS scheme in Goa would have been better. In this section I have tried to find out whether the monitoring authority had carried out the responsibilities assigned to it or not under this programme. This section includes the following information.

(i)   Taluka-wise staff working for the ICDS Programme in Goa.

(ii)   Number of meetings of the anganwadi workers held by the CDPOs in a month at the taluka level.

(iii) The number of times the Mukhya Sevikas (Supervisors) and the CDPOs visit the anganwadis in a month, talukawise.

(iv)   Total number of children enrolled under ICDS in 2001-02 and the annual total number of health check-ups carried out under each anganwadi in different talukas of Goa.

(v)   Age-group and educational qualification of the anganwadi workers under the ICDS Programme in Goa.

(vi)   Food eaten\not eaten by the anganwadi workers along with the children beneficiaries of ICDS Programme and proper pre-school education imparted\not imparted by the anganwadi workers.

(viii) The problems faced by the anganwadi workers of ICDS Programme in Goa.

(ix)   Some problems faced by the CDPOs of Goa.

The CDPOs of Goa have highlighted a few problems but the field survey of the anganwadis had brought out clearly the various other problems and their magnitude.

VI FINDINGS

The main findings are as follows.(1) All the children beneficiaries attending the anganwadis in Goa were within the prescribed age- limit of the ICDS Programme, majority of them came from low-income groups and 3.03% of the children beneficiaries were SC, 1.16% were ST, 36.13% were OBC and 59.67% belonged to the general category.(2) The majority of the children beneficiaries attending the anganwadis of Goa were Hindus.(3) The parents of the ICDS Programme beneficiaries were not highly qualified and some of them were illiterate.(4) It was seen that under the anganwadis 17.01% of the children beneficiaries were taken to the doctor 5 to 10 times annually before joining the ICDS Programme. After joining the ICDS Programme the number of children beneficiaries taken to the doctor increased.(5) The calorie intake of the children beneficiaries of the anganwadis under the ICDS Programme on four days of a week was far less than the normal requirements of 250 calories per day.(6) It was seen that 50.34% of the children beneficiaries under the anganwadis of Goa were not served food according to the timetable.(7) According to 32.16% of the parents of the beneficiaries of ICDS Programme their children did not long to go to the anganwadis, 11.18% of the parents of the children beneficiaries of the anganwadis felt that the anganwadi workers did not take care of the children and 30.76% of the parents of the beneficiaries felt that the anganwadi workers and helpers did not carry out their work and responsibility properly.(8) It was seen that 80.65% of the parents of the beneficiaries feel that no proper care was taken by the anganwadi workers to feed the children and 64.56% of the parents of the beneficiaries said that no proper non-formal pre-school teaching was imparted to children attending the anganwadis.(9) It was seen that 41.49% of the anganwadi workers and helpers did not follow strict working hours.Besides this, 25.49% of the anganwadi workers were absent between 10 to 20 days annually at the anganwadis.(10) Some of the children not belonging to the BPL (Below Poverty Line) were the beneficiaries of ICDS Scheme in Goa and many children remained absent at the anganwadis on the day of the field visit. (11)Some of the anganwadis in Goa lacked in basic amenities and infrastructure.(12)According to some of the parents of the beneficiaries, the selection of the anganwadi workers was done through pressure, anganwadi workers did not abide by the time schedules, there was pocketing of food stuff from the anganwadis, unhygienic anganwadis, congested rooms of the anganwadis, no proper records, no proper doors for the anganwadis etc.(13) There existed discrepancies in the allocation of Mukhya Sevikas under some of the talukas of Goa, discrepancies existed in the number of meetings of the anganwadi workers held in a month by the different Child Development Project Officers of Goa.(14) Some CDPOs did not make regular monthly visits to the anganwadis at the taluka level and there existed discrepancies in the number of visits made by the Mukhya Sevikas to the anganwadi centres.(15) There were irregular health checkups or no health checkups under the anganwadis of Goa. (16) Some of the anganwadi workers faced multiple problems like no proper storehouses, no proper transport facilities, very small rooms of the anganwadis, insects, no toys, no books, no charts, no slates, unhygienic place of location of the anganwadis, mud floors, no toilets, no electricity, etc. (17) Some anganwadi workers did not eat food along with the children beneficiaries of the anganwadis and 47.05% of the anganwadi workers did not impart proper pre-school education to the beneficiaries.(18) The CDPOs faced a number of problems like non-availability of official vehicle, political pressure to start new anganwadis, no proper office premises, etc.

(VII) CONCLUSIONS

(1) Only children from the prescribed age-groups availed the benefits of the anganwadis under the ICDS Programme in Goa. The majority of the beneficiaries came from low economic backgrounds and the Programme catered not only to the backward classes but majority of the beneficiaries belonged to the general category.(2) In Goa, Majority of the children beneficiaries attending the anganwadis were Hindus, which is probably due to higher percentage of Hindu population in Goa.(3) The educational family background of the ICDS beneficiaries attending the anganwadis in Goa was low, which added to low income earning capacities and low quality of life of the families, ignorance, carelessness, etc.(4) Even after attending the anganwadis and provision of supplementary food there was still no improvement

in the health of some of the ICDS beneficiaries which could be because of poor nutrition, lack of hygiene at the anganwadis, no proper infrastructure at the anganwadis, no proper storehouses for the foodgrains, leaking roofs during the rains, insects, rats, no proper kitchens, flies, no proper floors (potholes in the floors), mud floors, no toilets, no proper water supply facilities, no proper and timely medical checkups, no proper airy rooms, etc. This probably accounted for the increase in the number of their visits to the doctor per child after joining the anganwadis (5) The children beneficiaries of the anganwadis under the ICDS Programme in Goa did not get the adequate calorie intake of 250 calories on some days of the week, which is likely to affect the physical as well as the mental growth of children and also result in malnutrition of various grades. (6) Since majority of the children beneficiaries of ICDS Programme were not supplied food according to the timetable, it reflected the carelessness of the anganwadi workers and shortcomings in the working of the ICDS Programme in Goa. This also added to the problem of malnutrition, ill-health and it also affected the future labour force of our state.(7) Some of the anganwadi children did not like the environment of the anganwadis. The repulsive behaviour of some of the children towards the anganwadis could be because of lack of toys, serving of tasteless food, etc.(8) Some of the anganwadi workers did not have proper knowledge about childcare, they were ignorant, careless, and inefficient in their work, there was no accountability of their work, lack of monitoring by the higher authorities etc.(9) Many of the anganwadi centres lacked in books, there were no educative posters, etc.(10) There was absenteeism among the anganwadi workers, which affected the functioning of anganwadis in Goa.(11) There was absence of basic amenities under the anganwadis of Goa, which hindered the hygiene and sanitation. (12) There were various infrastructural problems, problems of inefficiencies by the anganwadi workers, inefficiencies in the selection of anganwadi workers, etc. which added to the overall mismanagement of the ICDS Programme in Goa. (13) The ICDS Scheme had failed in its objective of providing regular health checkups to its children beneficiaries. (14) There was no proper yardstick for the allocation of Mukhya Sevikas to different talukas according to the number of anganwadis in the talukas. There existed discrepancies in the allocation of staff at the taluka level under the ICDS Scheme in Goa. No proper strategies are laid down and followed. Besides this, there are faults in planning and implementation of the ICDS Programme in Goa. (15) The CDPOs of Goa under the ICDS Scheme did not carry out uniform number of meetings of the anganwadi workers at the taluka level. Besides this there existed taluka-wise discrepancies in the number of visits to the anganwadi centres made by the CDPOs and the Mukhya Sevikas of Goa during a month. The ICDS Scheme in Goa lacked uniformity in its functioning at the taluka level.(16) Lack of provision of official vehicle, additional charge\work, lack of accountability, etc resulted in inefficiency of some of the CDPOs and Mukhya Sevikas. (17) The anganwadi workers do not possess any specialized qualification\training in child-care, nutrition, hygiene, etc. (18)The ICDS Scheme in Goa also catered to people above the poverty line.(19) The anganwadi workers did not take up their responsibilities seriously. The multiple problems faced by anganwadi workers and the CDPOs affected the functioning of the Scheme in Goa.

VIII. RECOMMENDATIONS

The recommendations have been classified under the following heads.

(1) With regard to the programme

(i) For the success of any Programme the rules mentioned in the Programme should be strictly followed otherwise the non-target beneficiaries take the benefits of the Programme.

The Programme should cater to the right beneficiaries i.e. it should cater to the prescribed age-group\classes\categories only.(ii)Since the ICDS Programme in Goa is catering to the right beneficiaries and the economically backward families, it should continue in its functioning. However the quality of the programme should undergo a qualitative change with minimum drawbacks and efforts should be made to see that maximum benefits are got from this programme.(iii) Good care of children in the age-group of 0-6 years has to be taken, as these are the crucial years of development. Besides this, children of this age-group are susceptible to diseases\sickness very fast. Health of children in the age-group of 0-6 years should be protected as they represent a very important future labour force of the country. A country is said to be developed only if there are developments in its human resources. Sound health of children will lead to reduction in morbidity and mortality of children. There would be improvements in the mental and physical development of children, which in turn would lead to improvements in the quality of future labour resources of the country. The food that is supplied under the ICDS Programme to the children should be of better quality, should be in adequate calories and should be balanced. (iv) The central government should provide more funds for the ICDS Programme in Goa so as to improve its functioning and provide better nutrition and hygiene to the beneficiaries.(v)The anganwadi workers under the ICDS Programme in Goa should be adequately trained in various aspects of Child care, pre-school education, hygiene, health, child psychology etc.(vi) Under the ICDS Programme music, singing, dancing, playing, speaking, drawing, painting, craft, creative thinking, basic writing, acting, basic manners, proper habits etc. should be encouraged in the children by the anganwadi workers at different ages till they are 6 years of age. The ICDS Programme in Goa should be able to bring a qualitative change in Children who are the future labour force of the country. (vii) Proper detailed records should be maintained in registers about the government Programmes carried out.

(2) Monitoring authority.

The monitoring authorities of any programme should take their responsibilities very seriously. They should be well trained\ oriented to carry out their responsibilities. There should be better planning, management and accountaility of the work carried out by them. Periodic evaluation of the program with reference to the management of the programme should be done. Also periodic feedbacks should be collected by the monitoring authority so as to rectify any problems in the responsibilities carried out under the programme. Periodic evaluation of the programmes should be carried out by the monitoring authority so as to rectify any mistakes| discrepancies\irregularities in its functioning. This would ensure success of any programme to a large extent.

(3) Physical environment.

The anganwadis under the ICDS Programme in Goa should be provided with good physical environment with all basic amenities. A clean and congenial physical environment with all basic amenities should be provided to the children of the anganwadis so as to lead to good health and development of children physically as well as mentally.

(4) General

Only trained persons should carry out the survey and select genuine beneficiaries for any Programme.

(5) Society

The rural masses in general and the target group in particular must undertake the programme spontaneously and the beneficiaries should develop their attitude that these programmes belong to them rather than to the government.

References

Department of Women and Child Development, (1999), *Schemes for assistance: A handbook*, Government of Goa, New Delhi.

Directorate of Planning, Statistics and Evaluation (2006-07), *Economic Survey*, Government of Goa, Goa.

Directorate of Planning, Statistics and Evaluation (2007-08), *Economic Survey*, Government of Goa, Goa.

Directorate of Planning, Statistics and Evaluation (2008-09), *Economic Survey*, Government of Goa, Goa.

Directorate of Planning, Statistics and Evaluation (2009-10), *Economic Survey*, Government of Goa, Goa.

Directorate of Planning, *Statistics and Evaluation (2010-11)*, Economic Survey, Government of Goa, Goa.

Government of Goa, (1997), *Statistical handbook of Goa (1994-95 to 1996-97)*, Directorate of Planning, Statistics and Evaluation, Goa.

Government of India, (1999), Department of Women and Child development, Ministry of Human Resource Development.

Official records from the Integrated Child Development Services office, Valpoi Goa.

Official records from the RuralDevelopment Agency Office, Panaji- Goa.

Sengupta, G. (1988), *Welfare of women and children in West Bengal*, Ed. K. L. Bhowmik, Inter-India Publications, New Delhi.

6

SOCIO-ECONOMIC IMPACT OF TRADE UNIONS AT SELECTED UNITS IN GOA

*— Blanche R.C.S. Fernandes e Mascarenhas **

I. INTRODUCTION

Trade unions with their collective bargaining strength not only helps the workers and to improve their working conditions but also aid them and their families attain greater position as well as dignity in society. Trade unions have turned from the question of employment related issues to local concerns such as health, habitation, sanitation, and so on. Strong and healthy trade unions can contribute to improvements in labour productivity, economic development and also have a more determinate role to play in the process of adjustment and integration of the workers in the industrial life Socially too, unions enable masses of working population fulfill their aspirations than any other institution. In the organized sectors, trade unions not only take interest in solving problems of the workers, like health – care improvements, housing, family planning but at the same time in many cases, with their pressures, as also their constructive cooperation, have helped employers in undertaking programs for improving working efficiency of those units with benefits to employers, workers and the rest of the community. Activities like provision of canteens, encouragement of small savings through establishment

---

* *Associate Professor and Head, Department of Economics, St. Xavier's College, Goa*

of workers' credit societies, education in personal, social. and industrial hygiene, safety practices, child welfare, ensuring effective use of labour welfare centers and finally dissemination of general information to their members in order to create social awareness of their present day surroundings and the role expected of them in the tasks of national reconstruction and emotional integration have been undertaken by many trade unions during recent years.

II. THEORETICAL FRAMEWORK

Studies show that Unions play a strong role in bringing about improvements in conditions of work. Issues like equality of treatment at work or elimination of discrimination in hiring, promotions, transfers, provision of maternity benefits, transport, nature and amount of work along with wider issues having implications for the entire workforce were taken care of in their negotiations by the existing unions.

According to Robertson N & Thomas J.L. (1968), Trade unions aim to secure greater security for the workers – protect his job (against other workers, against redundancy) protect him when unemployed, sick, injured at work, etc. Trade unions were among the first institutions to provide social security to the working class. Originally, most forms of social insurance were offered by the unions. They also pressurized the State for social security policy formulation. Besides paying the social security benefits (both in cash & kind) they derive these benefits for the labour by the instrument of collective bargaining

Mahagaonkar N.S. (1986), shared that the trade unions also educate the workers for obtaining maximum benefits through social security schemes. Trade unions have a special role to play in the administration of social security measures –development and administration. Workers' nominees serve on the boards of many social insurance schemes. Indian unions provide legal aid to workers to avail the social security benefits as well as collectively bargain for the additional social security benefits from the employers.

Tiwari K. (1995) opined that the duty of a trade union is i) to educate and cooperate with the management to educate the employees regarding their duty with respect to safety and health, ii) participate in management 's efforts on training and supervising employees to follow safe and healthy working procedures and iii) cooperate with management in all bi-partite discussions on safety and health of employees.

Socially too, unions have a more determinate role to play in the lives of a vast mass of working population, and encompass more needs of the workers than any other institution.

Datar B.N.(1968), reported that in many cases, trade union pressures as also their constructive cooperation have helped employers in undertaking programs for improving working efficiency of those units with benefits to employers, workers and the rest of the community.

Ramaswamy U. (1983), pointed out that the social life of the workers is also influenced by the fact of industrial employment. Interpersonal relations in the community are also in many ways reflection of relations in the work sphere. Colleagues have intimate social relations, especially pronounced among union – activists. Union hostility and conflict are also taken home, although not with the same degree of intensity and loyalty. Union, work and political loyalties are sufficiently powerful as to considerably moderate the force of tradition in the social life of the community.

According to Khan W.M.R. (1985), trade unions play a very significant role in developing the labour community. Unions also assist in cultivation of proper food habits. In the organized sectors, trade unions take interest in solving housing problems of the workers, health –care improvements, family planning etc.

Goan Economy: An Analysis of Select Issues

According to Gupta A. (1992), the wages of the working class are of great importance to the workers and the society as a whole. Higher wages are an indication of the level of advancement and prosperity in the society. Wages determine the standard of living of the wage earner and his family. By bargaining for a better wage, the union aids the workers and their families to improve their size and nature of consumption and thus attain greater position, respect and dignity in society.

Joshi, R. J. (2007) stated that although most of the work conditions existed mainly due to management efforts, trade unions also have a special responsibility to take up issues with the management. Equality of treatment at work or elimination of discrimination in hiring, promotions, transfers, provision of maternity benefits, transport, along with wider issues having implications for the entire workforce were taken care of in their negotiations by the existing unions. Trade unions aim to secure greater security for the workers – protect his job (against other workers, against redundancy) protect him when unemployed, sick, injured at work, etc.

III. DATA AND METHODOLOGY

The study takes into account only the industrial trade unions in Goa. At present there are 114 industrial trade unions in Goa. For the purpose of this study, a sample of 5% of industrial unions have been selected through stratified sampling method. This 5% of trade unions selected i.e six unions are spread at the four units namely Mormugao Port Trust (MPT), Goa Shipyard Limited (GSL), Colfax Private Limited and Ciba Specialty Chemicals (India) Limited. The study covers the post liberalization period (1991-2005).

The distribution of these six unions are as follows: at MPT two unions have been studied namely Mormugao Port and Railway Workers Union (MPRWU) and Goa Port and

Dock Employees Union (GPDEU); at GSL two unions namely, Goa Shipyard Kamgar Sangh (GSKS) and Goa Shipyard Kamgar Ekvott (GSKE); at Colfax Private Limited one union namely Gomantak Mazdoor Sangh (GMS) and at Ciba Specialty Chemicals (India) Limited one union namely Kamgarancho Ekvott (KE). At these respective units, the total number of industrial unions existing at present which comprise the universe of the study is as follows: at MPT there are 10 trade unions, at GSL there are 3 trade unions, at Colfax there is one trade union and at Ciba there is one trade union.

However for the purpose of this study only recognized and viable unions in these units have been selected.

At MPT although the universe comprises of 10 unions, only two are recognized and viable. However, these cover 86% of the total number of workers (Class III + IV) at MPT, as most of the workers are members of these two unions. From these two unions, 5 % of the union members have been selected through stratified sampling method. At GSL, the universe comprises of 3 unions of which only two are recognized and viable. Here too, they cover 84% of the workers at GSL.

From these two, 5% of the union members have been selected. At Colfax, there is only one union and as it is a small unit, 50 % of the members of the union have been selected through stratified sampling method. At this unit every worker is a member of the union. At Ciba too, there is one union at present and as it is a small unit, 50 % of the members have been selected. They constitute 60% of the total workers at this unit. This paper seeks to examine the economic impact of Trade Unions with regard to Work Conditions, Job Security and Safety. The social impact will be examined with reference to Health and Welfare Measures, Standard of Living and Environment at these units.

IV. SOCIO-ECONOMIC IMPACT TRADE UNIONS AT MORMUGAO PORT TRUST

1. Economic Impact

(a) *Work Conditions:* With regard to fixing the length of the work - day and breaks, MPRWU favored increasing daily working hours to meet the required hours of work. At present they have settled for two five days week and two six days week for clerical, one hour lunch break for office staff and sub-sections while shift workers have built - in break timings. Improving service conditions have always been one of its priorities. GPDEU was actively involved with fixing the length of the workday and breaks as per the standing orders, shift changes and improvements in the work conditions. It accepted additional workload only if the workers were provided with incentives. The union is of the opinion that the facilities provided for workers and the physical work-environment was satisfactory and felt that the management was cooperative in nature.

(b) *Job Security:* GPDEU provides 100 % job security to its members according to its President. The union was successful in reinstating three termination cases. The union does not interfere with the employment policy of the unit but takes up grievances on matters regarding compensatory appointments. It objects transfers with low incentives, but allows transfers only under malpractice.

The MPRWU also provides job security to regular employees except those involved in disciplinary action, disobedience, thefts or other criminal cases. The union deals with maintaining seniority, cases arising on account of wrong fixation of wages as well as long term absenteeism. Since 1991 – 2005 no worker has been retrenched at MPT.

(c) *Safety:* Higher the number of accidents, lower will be

the safety of workers. Table 1. depicts the picture regarding accidents at MPT during 1991 - 2005.

Table 1

Particulars of Accidents: Causation & Number:

Year	Striking against objects				Falling of objects				Wrong move-ment				Caught in between				Person falling				Contact with electric Current				Run over				Others				Total	
	F		NF		F		NF		F		NF		F		NF		F		NF		F		NF		F		NF		F		NF		P	N
	P	N	P	N	P	N	P	N	P	N	P	N	P	N	P	N	P	N	P	N	P	N	P	N	P	N	P	N	P	N	P	N		
1990-91	-	-	3	1	-	-	-	4	-	-	-	-	-	-	1	-	-	1	-	-	-	-	-	-	-	-	-	-	-	-	-	-	4	6
1991-92	-	-	-	2	-	-	-	4	-	-	-	-	-	-	1	-	-	-	-	-	-	-	-	-	-	-	-	-	-	-	-	-	1	6
1992-93	-	-	1	4	-	-	-	3	-	-	1	-	-	-	-	1	-	-	-	1	-	-	-	-	-	-	-	-	-	-	1	-	3	9
1993-94	-	-	-	7	-	-	-	5	-	-	1	4	-	-	-	3	-	-	1	3	-	-	-	1	-	-	-	-	-	-	-	1	2	24
1994-95	-	-	1	3	-	-	-	5	-	-	3	3	-	-	-	1	-	-	4	-	-	-	5	-	-	-	-	-	-	2	-	-	13	14
1995-96	-	-	5	-	-	-	2	-	-	-	4	-	-	-	7	-	-	1	2	6	-	-	10	-	-	-	-	-	-	-	3	-	33	7
1996-97	-	-	4	1	1	-	8	-	-	-	2	-	1	-	1	1	-	-	-	1	-	-	7	-	-	-	-	-	1	-	1	-	26	3
1997-98	-	-	-	-	-	-	1	-	-	-	24	-	-	-	4	-	-	-	1	-	-	-	-	-	-	-	1	-	-	-	1	-	32	-
1998-99	-	-	12	-	-	-	1	-	-	-	-	-	-	-	2	-	-	-	5	-	-	-	-	-	1	-	-	-	-	-	1	-	22	-
1999-2000	-	-	5	-	-	-	1	-	-	-	1	-	-	-	2	-	1	-	6	-	-	-	1	-	-	-	-	-	-	-	-	-	17	-
2000-01	-	-	6	-	-	-	3	-	-	-	-	-	-	-	-	-	-	-	5	-	-	-	-	-	-	-	-	-	-	-	2	-	16	-
2001-02	-	-	2	-	-	-	3	-	-	-	-	-	-	-	1	-	-	-	6	-	-	-	1	-	1	-	-	-	-	-	2	-	16	-
2002-03	1	-	4	-	-	-	1	-	-	-	-	-	-	-	4	-	1	-	4	-	1	-	2	-	-	-	-	-	-	-	-	-	18	-
2003-04	1	-	8	-	-	-	2	-	-	-	-	-	-	-	1	-	-	-	2	-	-	-	1	-	1	-	-	-	-	-	-	-	16	-
2004-05	-	-	3	-	-	-	1	-	-	-	-	-	-	-	2	-	-	-	4	-	-	-	3	-	-	-	-	-	-	-	-	-	13	-

NB: *F = Fatal   NF = Non-Fatal   P = Port Area   N = Non-Port Area*
Source: *1. Annual Administrative Report of MPT, 1990 – 1991 to 2004 - 2005.*
2. Primary data collected through Interview with the Safety Officer.

It is evident from the figures given in Table 1. that from 1997 - 98 onwards there were no accidents reported at the Non Port Area. Striking against objects, falling of objects, caught in between and persons falling are yet major causes of accidents at the Port Area. Since 1998 – 99 onwards the number of accidents at the Port Area also have declined. According to both the unions, the management was reasonable in its provision for accidents and prevention of occupational diseases, but many workers were not making use of the safety devices, hence, the unions took interest in educating the workers regarding safety measures, by actively participating in the Safety Week, displaying posters and deputing two of its members for safety training every year.

Two representatives from each union were appointed to the safety committee since 1980 and from 2005, five representatives were appointed.

Table 2

Employees' Views regarding Job Security and Safety Devices

Sr. No	Item	MPRWU	GPDEU
1.	**Job Security** Present Absent No response	96.9 3.1 -	96.8 3.2 -
2.	**Safety Devices** Satisfactory Unsatisfactory No response	84.6 1.5 13.8	71.4 11.1 17.5
3.	**Met with an Accident** Yes No	15.4 84.6	14.3 85.7
4.	**Confidence in Leader** Yes No Partly No Response	55.4 30.8 7.6 6.2	100.0 - - -

Source: *Based on Primary data collected through Employee Questionnaires.*

Table 2 clearly shows that 96 % of the members of both the unions felt their jobs to be secure. According to MPRWU, 84 % were satisfied with safety devices and had never met with an accident at work, but only 55 % had confidence in the union leader. With reference to GPDEU, even though only 71 % were satisfied with safety devices and about 14 % had met with an accident at work, all the members had confidence in their leader.

Social Impact

The unions at MPT also performed the following social functions:

(a) *Health and Welfare:* As a measure to promote health of the workers, the management runs a 100 bedded hospital, a first aid center, a primary health center, conducts periodic health check-ups, health camps, educative programmes, medical benefits after retirement, counseling etc.

With reference to promotion of health, the role of the two unions at MPT, can be summarized as follows:

GPDEU contributed towards the promotion of health facilities in the following ways:
- taking up cases with referral to other hospitals for specialized treatment - TATA, KAD Belgaum.
- demanded amendment of medical regulations.
- staged demonstrations for removal of garbage.
- objected to the contributive medical benefits scheme for pensioners and asked for free treatment.
  While MPRWU
- amended medical attendance regulations to enable patients to go for specialized treatment outside the state.
- extended the family benefits to in-laws as well.

- disabled children of employees brought under medical benefits. (until death)
- demanded provision of medical benefits after retirement.

Secondly, the Port Administration continued its efforts to better welfare amenities to the employees and extend assistance in promoting the all-round growth of employees and their families. It runs primary, secondary and high secondary schools, vocational center, provides scholarships, housing, canteens, transport facilities; the expenses on which are shown in Table 3.

Table 3

Break up of total expenses on welfare measures (in Rs. Crs)

Year	Exp on Hospital	Bus trans	Transport re-imbursement	Welfare expenses (from welfare Fund)	Scholarships/ edu.allow,/ fees/welfare/ grants/sport/ small fly incentive/ welfare buildings ,etc	Maintenance of staff quarters	LTC	Subsidy to Canteen	Total
1990-91				270.53					
1991-92				332.70					
1992-93				431.436					
1993-94				495.704					
1994-95		45.40	11.74		63.49	57.35	9.46	1.98	189.42
1995-96		48.27	9.41		69.67	68.74	6.30	2.19	204.58
1996-97	na	Na	na	Na	na na	na		Na	na
1997-98	333.44	58.23	35.35	3.55	166.24 127.33	9.17		2.41	736.85
1998-99	391.68	64.69	-	3.74	189.27 141.77	31.95		3.04	861.63
1999-00	478.47	63.83	35.23	15.00	162.75 190.06	36.05		4.93	986.92
2000-01	620.60	89.93	73.42	3.88	148.83 141.53	15.08		7.32	1100.44
2001-02	613.86	90.05	-	7.18	128.87			8.15	848.11
2002-03	640.60	99.23	-	6.78	348.86			8.30	1103.77
2003-04	648.73	94.39	-	8.05	311.56			7.74	1070.47
2004-05	600.97	80.00	-	5.00	300.89			12.0	1100.83

Source: Annual Administrative Report of MPT, 1990-1991 to 2004-2005.

Regarding MPRWU, since 1990-95, three members were appointed as representatives to the welfare committee, but during 1995-2004 no representative was appointed. However from 2005, one union representative was appointed to this committee. In addition it tried to settle family problems, provided guidance on loans and its payments, counseling services, visited families of its members and conducted widow re-marriages (six members).

GPDEU had no representation to the welfare committee and yet it tried to promote welfare of its members. It brought award of scholarships from Jawaharlal Nehru Port Trust and also introduced Tuition Fee Re-imbursement based on Tuticorin Port Trust.

(b) *Standard of Living:* The unions worked to improve the standards of living of its members and their families by raising wages and allowances, productivity linked incentives and demanding provision of better housing, health, transport, education and recreational facilities by the management.

(c) *Environment / Area Development Program :* The Port has adopted several measures for the improvement of the environment within the operational areas such as a) Creation of special Cell to monitor the level of pollution. b) Plantation of 1000 samplings on the periphery of the Port Security wall, to trap dust. c) Wet dust suppression system. d) Regular spraying of water on roads. e) Mechanical road sweeper. f) Covering of all trucks and rail wagons during transportation of cargo out of the port. g) Introduction of sprinkling towers.

The unions too showed an increasing interest in caring for the environment. GPDEU held dharnas for environment cleaning, while the leader of MPRWU was appointed as a member of the Port Operating Group that discussed issues like cleanliness, hygiene, environmental issues and suggested measures for its improvement.

V. SOCIO-ECONOMIC IMPACT OF TRADE UNIONS AT GOA SHIPYARD LIMITED

Economic Impact

(a) *Work Conditions:* Even though one of the unions expressed that the management satisfactorily catered to the legitimate physical, medical and psychological needs of the workers, the other union negated the same and demanded improvement of working conditions at GSL, as majority of its members found most of them to be unsatisfactory.

(b) *Job Security:* GSKS gave first preference to promotion policy. Secondly it suggested appointment of tradesmen / new employees to fill the 500 vacant posts caused by VRS, which at present are being filled by contract workers. GSKE succeeded in reinstating a worker who was dismissed even though the worker was not its member. No worker has been dismissed because of absenteeism.

(c) *Safety:* GSKS demanded goggles, hand gloves, helmets, shoes and training of batches of workers in first aid and safety.

GSKE got the management to appoint the Promotion Policy Review Committee. The union opines that the management has not been reasonable in its provision for accidents and prevention of occupational diseases. The union gave more emphasis to provision of Safety training and First aid workshops.

Table 4

Number of Accidents, Workers involved and Man days lost during 1991-2005.

Year	No.of accidents	No. of workers involved	No. of man days lost
1991	5	5	59
1992	6	6	74
1993	8	7	132
1994	8	9	109
1995	27	26	662
1996	14	21	303
1997	10	6	69
1998	9	9	202
1999	27	21	411
2000	27	32	490
2001	23	26	399
2002	22	26	371
2003	8	9	160
2004	17	16	199
2005	25 (UPTO OCT)	25	290

Source: *Primary data collected through Management Questionnaire.*

It is evident from Table 4, that there were greatest number of accidents recorded during 1995 with a loss of 662 man days. Equivalent number of accidents were reported in 1999 and 2000 (but with less man days lost) followed by a decline in number thereafter, but shows a rise from 2004 onwards.

Table 5.

Employees' Views regarding Job Security and Safety Devices

Sr. No	Item	GSKS	GSKE
1.	**Job Security** Present Absent No response	82.6 13.0 4.3	95.5 4.5 -
2.	**Safety Devices** Satisfactory Unsatisfactory	78.3 21.7	68.2 31.8
3.	**Met with an Accident** Yes No	8.7 91.3	40.9 59.1
4.	**Confidence in Leader** Yes No	82.6 17.4	100.0 -

Source: *Based on Primary data collected through Employee Questionnaires*

Table 5, shows that 82 % members of GSKS were of the opinion that job security was prevalent and had confidence in their leader, while 21 % members were unsatisfied with the safety devices although, less than 10 % had met with an accident at the work place. Secondly, 95 % members of GSKE felt their jobs to be secure. About 40 % members had met with an accident at the work place and only 68 % were satisfied with the safety devices, and hence felt unsafe. All members had confidence in their leader.

Social Impact

(a) *Health and Welfare:* GSKS demanded a common Medical Scheme for workers and supervisors. It advised it members on Aids and its preventive measures. In addition, it suggested health awareness programmes and reduction of oily food served at the canteen as, on an average the workers are above 40 yrs of age and face cholesterol problem. Under the Death Benefit Welfare Fund, the family of the deceased gets Rs. 20,000 for which the worker contributed Rs. 4/- per month. The union suggested that it was ready to contribute Rs. 8/- and the benefit should be raised to Rs. 40,000. The union also advised its members on the provident fund and pension benefits.

The president of the union has worked as the Director of the Cooperative Store and at present as its Vice-President. As a chief promoter of the Co-operative Credit Society, he took the initiative to register the same in 1986, and has been working continuously as its Secretary for the last 10 years.

Although GSKE did not conduct any welfare activity for the workers, its President proudly asserts that most of the welfare measures present at GSL were demanded by the union, and got implemented by the management. Its demands included Child education allowance, Dispensary, Workers' education programmes and in-house training related to workers' trade.

(b) *Standard of Living:* In the opinion of GSKS, the standard of living differed between workers due to the difference in skill, wages and consumption levels.

Both the unions paid special attention to advising its members regarding reduction in consumption, being regular to work, giving up alcoholism. It also demanded improvement in wages, health and welfare amenities, educational facilities provided by the management, so as to improve the status of its members and their families as well.

(c) *Environment / Area Development Program:* GSKE actively participated in the Civic administration. It took up the clearing of the nullah and also the initiative to sponsor the road divider at Swatantra path.

VI. SOCIO-ECONOMIC IMPACT OF TRADE UNIONS AT COLFAX PRIVATE LIMITED

Economic Impact

(a) *Work Conditions*: Sixty percent of the negotiations by the union were related to the prevailing working conditions. By and large, through negotiations, the union has been able to improve the work conditions satisfactorily.

(b) *Job Security:* The union is presently representing two cases in court. Secondly the union sees that after ten years of service, the workers are entitled for promotion and in cases where workers performed high quality work are immediately promoted.

(c) *Safety:* The union was satisfied with the provision of measures regarding accidents and occupational disease prevention by the management.

Table 6

Employees' Views regarding Job Security and Safety Devices

87.5	Item	GMS
12.5	**Job Security** Present Absent	100.0 -
2.	**Safety Devices** Satisfactory Unsatisfactory	95.8 4.2
3.	**Met with an Accident** Yes No	29.2 70.8
4.	**Confidence in Leader** Yes No	87.5 12.5

Source: *Based on Primary data collected through Employee Questionnaires.*

It is evident from Table 6, that 30 % of the members had met with an accident during work, 95 % were satisfied with safety devices and 87 % had confidence in their leader. During the 1994 blast at the unit which caused the death of 6 workers, the union attended the funeral by representation, and kept the unit functioning and paid one day extra payment to the deceased family. The union saw that compensation as well as job to the deceased family member was provided by the management.

Social Impact

According to the General Secretary of GMS, it restricted its functioning to the economic aspects only, as the social measures were found to be satisfactory at the unit and indirectly tried to improve the status of its members.

VII. SOCIO- ECONOMIC IMPACT OF TRADE UNIONS AT CIBA SPECIALTY CHEMICALS (INDIA) LIMITED

Economic Impact

(a) *Work Conditions:* The union does not allow increase in workdays as well as decrease in breaks. It was also against any change in service conditions unless it is discussed and settled with the union. Improvements in facilities for workers have been constantly demanded by the union. It kept a constant watch on the physical work environment and worked to improve the same.

(b) *Job Security:* The union did not allow termination of services of any of its members. It opposed labour saving technical change and approved technical change that leads to progress, provided workers' interests were protected.

(c) *Safety:* The union was satisfied with the provision for accidents and prevention of occupational diseases.

Table 7.

Employees' Views regarding Job Security and Safety Devices

87.5	Item	KE
12.5	**Job Security** Present Absent	100.0 -
2.	**Safety Devices** Satisfactory Unsatisfactory	92.9 7.1
3.	**Met with an Accident** Yes No	0.0 100.0
4.	**Confidence in Leader** Yes No	92.9 7.1

Source: *Based on Primary data collected through Employee Questionnaires.*

Table 7 proves that majority of the workers felt safe, secure and had confidence in their leader.

Social Impact

According to the General Secretary of the union, it did not undertake any social functions, but aimed at improving the standard of living of its members indirectly. He strongly believed that a rise in the earnings of the workers improves their standard of living.

VII. CONCLUSION

From the analysis of data with regard to the socio-economic role of the trade unions in the four units studied, we conclude that all the unions in the units under study have played a significant role in improving the work conditions, job security and safety of the workers to a great extent as well as health and welfare, standard of living, environmental care to some extent by some of the unions. We can conclude that trade unions are not only performing economic functions, but also social functions. The unions have realised that for the wholesome development of the worker, they cannot restrict themselves to only improving the economic aspect of the workers' lives, but that the social aspect has to also be improved simultaneously. This will have long term repercussions in enhancing the productivity of the workers, thus benefiting the employers and society at large.

References

Datar B.N. (1968). *Labour Economics,* Allied Publishers, New Delhi.

Joshi R.J. (2007), "Quality of Work Life of Women Workers: Role of Trade Unions", *Indian Journal of Industrial Relations,* Vol 42, No. 3, January.

Khan W.M.R. (1985). A Study of Trade Unionism in shops & Commercial Establishments in Pune City, Department of Commerce, Ness Wadia College of Commerce, Pune.

Kumar A. (1999), " major issues before trade unions in India: Need to reorient demands", *The Indian Journal of Labour Economics,* Vol. 42, No. 4, October-December.

Mahagaonkar N.S. (1986). Role of Trade Unions in Labour Welfare, Briham Maharastra College of Commerce, Pune.

Mormugao Port Trust Annual Administrative Reports of 1991 to 2005

Ramaswamy U. (1983). *Work, Union and Community- Industrial Man in South India.*

Roy S.D. (2002), " Job Security Regulations & Worker Turnover: A study of the manufacturing sector", *Indian Economic Review,* Vol. XXXVII, No.2.

Sham Sundar K.R. (2006), " Changing Labour Institutions", *Economic and Political Weekly,* Vol. XLI, No. 3, January.

Tiwari, K. (1995). Absenteeism and Industrial Development. Causes, Impact and Control Measures. New Delhi. Deep and Deep Publishers.

7

PRODUCT PROFILE AND MARKET ANALYSIS OF THE PHARMACEUTICAL COMPANIES REGISTERED IN GOA

— *Anna Rovina Fernandes** — *Silvia M. Noronha***

I. INTRODUCTION

The small state of Goa, one of the major tourist destinations in India, is also a major pharmaceutical producer in the country with an annual production of over Rs. 2000 crore. Goa caters to nearly 12 per cent of the country's total pharma produce i.e. one-tenth of the total pharmaceuticals manufactured in the country. As per official figures, Goa has 295 registered pharmaceutical producers together with 403 units in operation, including loan-licensed units. Of this 108 are independent units. While most units undertake manufacturing of various pharma products, some have also set up R&D centres. Goa's pharma hub employs more than 10,000 persons directly and several thousands indirectly as well.

The intensity of competition among the pharmaceutical companies in Goa is rapidly increasing and the market environment for the smaller local companies can be characterized as volatile, and complex. Recent health care trends in India are posing new challenges as well as offering opportunities for increasing profitability. Certain therapeutic segments in the pharmaceutical

* *Assistant Professor in Economics, Carmel College, Nuvem-Goa*
** *Professor & Head, Department of Economics, Goa University*

market such as antibiotics, vitamins and minerals substitutes, cholesterol-reducers, anti-infectives etc. are on an upward swing. This presents a potential opportunity to pharma companies to improve their sales and profitability.

The challenge before pharmaceutical marketers is how to capitalize on the expanded market opportunities in the growing therapeutic segments. Adding to this challenge is the fact that due to the introduction by companies of several substitute drugs in the same product category, commonly referred to as 'me-too-drugs', the market in the same segment becomes highly fragmented. The challenge before each pharmaceutical company then, is to develop a strategic marketing plan that will create trust, affinity and loyalty of physicians to its product or products.

II. OBJECTIVES AND METHODOLOGY

The objective of this paper is to study the product profile of the pharmaceutical companies registered in Goa. The paper aims to analyze the market for the chosen therapeutic categories and the marketing plan of each company. The study will determine how in a highly competitive situation, the companies plan and manage the products to retain or expand their market share.

The study covers the pharmaceutical companies that are registered with the Registrar of Companies, Govt. of Goa, under the Companies Act, and accordingly have their registered headquarters in Goa. The selected companies are: i) Wallace Pharmaceuticals Pvt. Ltd. ii) Cosme Farma Laboratories Ltd. iii) Kare Pharmaceuticals Pvt. Ltd. iv) Geno Pharmaceuticals Ltd. v) Merit Pharmaceuticals Pvt. Ltd. vi) Goa Antibiotics and Pharmaceuticals Limited. vii) Toyo Laboratories Private Limited.

Primary data has been collected by administering a questionnaire to the Directors/ General Managers/ Marketing Heads of selected companies and by using the personal interview method.

The study covers the time period from 2002-2007. Secondary Data pertaining to the companies for the period 2002-07, has been obtained from Annual Reports of the companies, obtained from the Registrar of Companies, Goa for the stated period.

III. OVERVIEW OF LITERATURE

Reekie(1971), gives many empirical examples to show that introduction of new products or 'augmentation' in existing products can be used by pharmaceutical companies not only offensively to expand company sales in new and existing market segments but can also be used as a defensive marketing strategy to protect existing market share. The other factors according to him, that lead to higher market share are product quality and product characteristics and 'positioning' products in a particular market by making claims as to the uses of the product.

Smith (1983), in a review of various therapeutic classes found out that large initial promotion expenditures are a prerequisite for achieving a significant market share with a new product. He pointed out that pharmaceutical manufacturers aim to reduce the level of promotional support they give to individual products over time. For established products, the optimum level of promotional expenditure generally depends on a number of factors including the current market share, the market growth rate, competitor's promotion expenditure, the extent of brand switching and new product activity. His analysis of patterns of promotional expenditure within a therapeutic class is suggestive of an 'optimum' level of promotional expenditure for an individual product. He concludes that a "threshold level" of promotional expenditure exists for new as well as established products, depending on factors like therapeutic class and the size of the target group of doctors. Companies spending below this threshold level would be wasting promotional expenditure as it will be ineffective.

Smarta (1994) is of the view that since it is difficult for smaller pharmaceutical companies to come up with new drug discovery and development, they should engage in "Product Augmentation", rather than just churning out innumerable brands without any product differentiation. Product Augmentation is the voluntary improvement brought about in the product by the manufacturer. This is essentially to create a significant, meaningful and perceivable differentiation in the product. This augmentation can be created in the basic product itself or in the packaging or by creating differentiation in the manufacturing process. The extra plus of the product should then be communicated effectively. He further suggests that the product profile of a pharmaceutical company should enable it to attain all or a few of these objectives; growth, survival, resource utilization, stability in sales, profit and return on investment, flexibility to adapt to changing customers needs and profit. He points out that product policy and strategy affects a company's future significantly. The choice of products of a firm influences all the other elements in its marketing programme and has significant implications for such functional areas as Finance, Production and Personnel. He refers to product policy and strategy as the 'micro-marketing functions' that influences a firm's marketing strategy and management.

IV. PRODUCT PROFILE OF THE SELECTED COMPANIES

Smaller Indian pharmaceutical companies have a presence in 'branded formulations' category of pharmaceutical products largely in the domestic and a few semi-regulated markets abroad. Companies that are able to update their products portfolios in line with the therapeutic needs of the market, experience more robust earnings growth. Having a strong product pipeline is essential to sustain future earnings for a pharmaceutical company. It is also critical for those targeting exports to regulated markets to maintain systems and processes that ensure product quality.

Understanding the disease pattern in the targeted markets is important for the smaller pharmaceutical companies. This will enable them to judge the potential of the market for each category of drugs and to identify the marketing opportunities in order to form a strategic market plan.

The range of products manufactured by the seven companies registered in Goa, were classified under certain broad therapeutic categories. Product categories are than ranked on the basis of maximum number of companies producing products within a certain therapeutic category. Table 1 shows the product categories to which the products manufactured by the selected companies belong and their ranking in terms of number of companies producing them. A score of 7 would indicate that all seven companies produce in that category and hence the category will occupy the first rank.

Table 1

The Distribution of Product Categories among the Selected Companies.

Product Category	Score	Percentage of firms producing	Ranking
Antibiotic and antibacterial	7	100	1
Vitamin Preparations	6	85.7	2
Anti-inflammatory / analgesics	7	100	1
Cough and cold preparations	7	100	1
Dermatological	4	57.1	4
Gynecological	3	42.8	5
Anti-asthmatics	4	57.1	4
Anti-diabetics	3	42.8	4
Anti-vertigo	3	42.8	5
Cardio-vascular	2	28.5	6
Nutritional supplements	2	28.5	6
Psychotrophics	5	71.4	3
Anti-histamines	3	42.8	5

Source: *Calculated from primary data.*

In the analysis of product portfolios of the selected pharmaceutical companies, it is observed that antibiotics, antibacterial, anti-inflammatory and analgesics, and cough and cold preparations occupy the first position, being manufactured by all the selected pharmaceutical companies. These are segments with high growth in demand as the main disease patterns observed are mostly due to bacterial infections. There are various seasonal appearances of bacterial infections and gastro-intestinal disorders among the people in India. The most common bacterial infections are upper and lower respiratory tract infections and urinary tract infections. In addition to these, malaria and hepatitis are also common. (Health Condition Reports, GOI). The pharmaceutical companies under study cater to these emerging needs, by manufacturing a range of products.

The cough and cold preparation is the other therapeutic category with products manufactured by all the seven pharmaceutical players.

There is an increased demand from this segment, as urbanization and accompanying environmental pollutants result in infections.Anti-inflammatory and analgesics also occupy a very significant position in product portfolio of the selected companies, the demand of which is also high in India due to a transition to a stressful urban lifestyle.

Vitamin preparations are manufactured by six of the seven selected companies. Demand for these exists, because after every dose of antibiotics, which reduces the patients body resistance, doctors, prescribe a regimen of vitamin supplements. Psychotropic drugs which are administered for hypertension, depression and other neurological disorders also form an important component of the product portfolio of selected companies. Anti-asthmatics, anti-diabetics and dermatologicals are manufactured by four of the seven companies. Three companies produce gynaecologicals, anti-vertigo and anti-histamines while only two companies produce cardiovascular products.

A study of the product profile of the selected companies reveals the following:

1. The existing product categories are high demand segments as evident from emerging disease patterns.

2. However, there is concentration of production among the selected companies in the same therapeutic segments.

3. The pharmaceutical companies under study do not have a presence in the high value therapeutic segments like cardiovascular, ophthalmology, neurology and other specialty segments.

It can be inferred from the above that very small local pharmaceutical companies will find it extremely difficult to face competition in these segments which are flooded by substitute products of domestic and MNC companies. Companies need to have innovative skills of 'Product augmentation' based on qualitative improvements and strong marketing capabilities to create an image for their brands. Although operating under highly competitive conditions, the demand pattern in the chosen therapeutic categories offer high potential for growth in sales volume, so that with right marketing skills, market sustenance is possible even for the smaller companies.

Many of these companies are found to be supplementing their market earnings by manufacturing on loan license basis for other companies. It can be inferred from this that inorder to survive the big competition through such opportunities, the companies should ensure that their manufacturing laboratories, testing and analytical equipment and storage conditions are of high standards. The manufacturing plants of the small units like Merit do not have GMP certification. They are constrained by the shortage of financial resources and require government support for up gradation of their technological capabilities to become GMP compliant. This is crucial for their image building and future survival.

V. PRODUCT PROFILE AND MARKET ANALYSIS: A COMPARATIVE STUDY OF THE SELECTED COMPANIES

i) Comparative Manufacturing Capabilities

In the present competitive regime, inadequacies of capital, technology and skills are found to be affecting the market prospects of the small pharmaceutical companies in Goa. A comparative look at the levels of fixed capital investments of the firms will provide insights into the manufacturing capabilities and market standing of the companies.

Table 2

Fixed Capital Investments of Selected Companies in Goa as on March, 2007

(Rs.in lakhs)

Category	Geno	Wallace	Kare	Toyo	Merit	CFL	GAPL
Land and Building	407	1175.04	430	-	3.34	630.66	151.70
Plant and Machinery	132.66	477.39	44.16	0.71	9.78	66.90	175.18
QualityControl	8.82	49.40	72.20	0.32	-	-	22.26
R&D	56	172.57	15.00	-	-	43.28	-
Other fixed Expenses	412.67	2068.44	424 28	1.76	3.67	194.95	48.96
TOTAL	**1017.15**	**3942.84**	**985.64**	**2.79**	**16.79**	**935.79**	**398.10**

Source- *Data obtained from Annual Reports of given companies*

It can be noted from the table that Geno and Wallace has fixed capital investments of more than Rs.10 crore, while Kare and Cosme Farma records fixed investments worth Rs. 9 crore. GAPL has fixed investments worth 3 crore, while Toyo and Merit are very small units in terms of fixed capital investments.It is mandatory for the firms to invest in quality control but the level of capital investment in quality control processes and systems in case of the small units is very low. R&D investments of the large and medium sized units are focused on enhancing the quality of formulations and is called as 'formulations' R&D. Pooling of the R&D resources by the units through collaborations and establishing links with academic research institutes could result in more value additions to their research efforts.

The pharmaceutical firms are required to comply with Good Manufacturing Practices (GMP) norms as laid down by the World Health Organization. Fulfillment of this norm is mandatory for obtaining registrations of products abroad. A State GMP certificate is a must to participate in Government tenders.

Table 3

Status of Selected Companies in terms of GMP certification

WHO-GMP certified plants	Plant without GMP certification
Geno	Merit
Wallace	Toyo(State GMP)
CFL	
Kare	
GAPL	

Source: *Primary data obtained from companies*

It is to be noted that Merit Pharmaceuticals is constrained by shortage of financial resources and require Governmental support for upgradation of its infrastructure to become GMP compliant. This is also crucial if it is to survive in future on the basis of contract manufactuaring.

ii) Comparative Analysis of Market Performance of the Selected Companies

Effectiveness of Marketing Representatives(MRs) is critical to building company's image in the minds of the doctors. However the smaller companies expressed difficulties in retaining good

MRs, who they say get trained with a smaller company and then switch over to a larger company. On.y 2 of the 7 firms under study agreed that a highly competent MR working for a less known company may not be as successful as a less competent MR working for a well known company.

Table 4
Number of Medical Representatives employed by the selected   Companies-(2006-07)

Firms	Nos.
Geno	491
Wallace	440
CFL	850
Kare	75
Toyo	18
Merit	30

Source: *Primary data*

Cosme Farma has substantially increased the number of medical representatives over the years and has been incurring high expenses on its field force staff. The smaller of the companies have fewer medical representatives.

The management personnel of these companies pointed out that reducing sales force to cut down costs is not possible as direct mailing to doctors does not have the desired impact.

Table 5
Trends in Marketing Expenditure (Percentage of total expenditure)

Firms	2000-01	2001-02	2002-03	2003-04	2004-05	2005-06
Geno	21.42	22.01	21.63	21.75	23.92	23.82
Wallace	30	30	30	30	30	30
CFL	23	23	23	23	23	23
Kare	35	30	25	25	20	20
Toyo	40	38	35	30	30	28
Merit	25	25	25	25	25	25

Source: *Primary Data obtained from companies.*

Geno spent on an average 22.42 per cent of its total expenditure on marketing over the six year period. Wallace, CFL, and Merit maintained that they have consistently spent 30, 23 and 25 percents respectively of their total expenditure on marketing over the same period; Kare and Toyo are found to have decreased their marketing expenditures over the same period.

The firms under study have a very small share in the total pharmaceutical market as can be seen in Table 6.

Table 6
Overall Domestic Market Share of the Selected Companies.

Firms	MARKET SHARE (PERCENTAGE)
Geno	0.5
CFL	0.3
WAL-LACE	0.5
KARE	0.3
Toyo	0.03
Merit	0.001

Source: *Primary data obtained from companies.*

The bigger companies need to be more innovative in their marketing techniques and may have to allocate a higher proportion of their revenues in marketing activities. The smaller firms are constrained in their marketing efforts by the lack of resources and need to be brought under the cluster development programme by the Government to provide them comprehensive support. Wallace, CFL, Geno and Kare are actively pursuing export opportunities as shown in table 7. However, it is noted that Toyo and Merit are constrained by inadequate investment and lack of knowledge of export markets and limit themselves to sales within the country only. Although GAPL has manufacturing capabilities, it does not have the ability to compete in the market and largely relies on institutional sales.

Table 7
Target Markets of Selected Companies

FIRMS	Target Markets Abroad	Domestic Markets
Geno	Nepal, Africa, South-East Asia	Rural and Urban markets in India
Wallace	Tanzania, Kenya, Guyana, Sri-Lanka	Rural and Urban Markets in India
CFL	Mauritius, Kenya, Srilanka, Jamaica	Rural and Urban Markets in India
Kare	Nepal, SriLanka, Malaysia, Honduras, Phillipines, Vietnam	Rural and Urban Markets in India
Toyo	-	- Goa, Kerala, Karnataka, Maharashtra
Merit	-	- Goa, Kerala, Karnataka, Maharashtra,
GAPL	-	Institutional Market in India

Source: *Primary Data obtained from Companies.*

From the comparative analysis of companies, it can be stated that low-cost manufacturing capability is their key strength; however, it is critical for those targeting exports to regulated markets to maintain systems and processes that ensure product quality. This calls for greater levels of investments in upgradation of manufacturing infrastructure, testing facilities, storage and quality control systems. Levels of investments in R&D are also crucial for enhancing the product manufacturing process, product quality, and product benefits. This implies that Government of Goa should treat the small scale formulations units as a separate entity and help them to sustain in the competitive environment by a series of measures. The clustering approach where all small and medium units are considered as one cluster for which there should be well implemented measures to provide technological upgradation and marketing support will go a long way in ensuring the market presence of these firms.

iii) Comparative Analysis of the Promotional and Distributional Practices of the Companies Under Study.

The comparison between the seven companies is undertaken on the basis of the total promotional and distributional expenditure incurred by them and expressed as a percentage of total sales. Companies are also ranked on the basis of average sales turnover for the period from 2002-03 to 2006-07 and on the basis of average profitability. Profit after tax is taken into account to compare profitability.

A comparative picture of the amount spent by the selected companies on sales promotion and advertisements, excluding field force incentives is shown in table 8.

Table 8

Relative expenditure of companies on sales promotion and advertisement (expressed as percentage of sales)

Year	Geno	Wallace	Kare	Cosme Farma	Toyo	Merit	GAPL
\multicolumn{8}{l}{Expenditure incurred by}

Year	Geno	Wallace	Kare	Cosme Farma	Toyo	Merit	GAPL
2002-03	4.2	2.6	0.6	6.7	1.0	2.4	0.09
2003-04	3.7	2.2	0.1	3.0	1.7	2.7	0.08
2004-05	4.0	2.5	0.1	2.2	1.1	1.2	0.07
2005-06	5.5	2.9	0.1	1.1	1.0	1.8	0.01
2006-07	3.9	4.3	0.1	0.8	1.8	1.6	0.06

Source: Calculated figures from company reports.

The companies that allot a relatively higher amount on sales promotion are Geno, Cosme Farma and Wallace, while the companies spending, the least are Kare and GAPL. It is to be noted that these two companies i.e. Kare and GAPL, have been incurring losses. Average expenditure has been 4.2, 2.9 and 2.7 for Geno, Wallace and CFL respectively. The proportion of expenditure incurred by the companies on sales promotion is dependent on factors like stages of the product life cycle to which the core products belong, expenditure necessary to be incurred on salaries, incentives and allowances to field staff and on distribution, competitor's activities, company goals and objectives. It is noted that CFL has reduced expenditure on sales promotion and advertisement over the period, as company sources state that expenditure on field force staff comprised the major chunk of total marketing expenditure.

Major distribution costs incurred by the companies include expenditure on transportation, commissions to C&F agents and agency expenses and other administrative overheads.Only Geno pharmaceuticals has its own sales depot and has appointed C&F agents, while Kare entrusts its distribution function to Kare Health Specialties Ltd., a specialized company of the Kare group. Wallace, CFL, Toyo and Merit have appointed C & F agents to look after logistics and physical distribution. These intermediaries are paid a certain percentage of sales as commission. The system of appointing C & F agents has helped these companies to considerably reduce the depot management expenses and field force can concentrate on promotion of the products instead of wasting time on logistics. In addition to the commission paid to the agent, companies bear other additional expenses like transport costs, handling and communication expenses.

Table 9

Relative expenditure of companies on major distributional heads. (expressed as percentage of sales)

Expenditure incurred by							
Year	Geno	Wallace	Kare	CFL	Toyo	Merit	GAPL
2002-03	8.9	3.7	1.5	1.1	4.0	1.7	7.1
2003-04	8.1	3.4	1.5	1.1	3.9	2.0	5.3
2004-05	8.0	3.8	1.2	2.3	4.6	3.4	2.3
2005-06	8.3	3.7	0.8	2.0	4.9	1.6	0.8
2006-07	8.3	4.2	2.5	1.9	5.4	1.9	0.9

Source: *Estimated values based on company reports.*

It appears from table 9 that Geno pharmaceuticals has scope to economize on its distributional overheads, while the other companies have to evolve policies to optimize their distributional budget. Companies should explore techniques of distribution management and optimization. Arriving at an optimal distribution system requires in-depth cost-benefit analysis by each of the companies. Ensuring that there are no stock-outs of company products is another challenge before the pharmaceutical companies.

iv) Comparative Trends in Sales and Profits

Table10

Sales (expressed in lakh rupees)

Year	Geno	Wallace	Kare	Cosme	Toyo	Merit	GAPL
2002-03	4193.31	10579.24	1695.60	7283.49	75.70	62.08	2430.65
2003-04	5132.15	12163.78	1708.75	8558.85	75.71	71.40	1787.05
2004-05	5088.35	9672.23	1516.20	8388.73	74.51	71.44	1007.38
2005-06	6551.00	13018.51	2483.40	10668.67	101.21	89.54	1067.69
2006-07	8012.17	13820.74	1642.83	12524.72	106.03	89.85	1076.33

Source: *Company Annual Reports*

The comparative trends in sales reveals that Wallace, Cosme Farma and Geno have achieved positive growth in sales over the years, except in 2004-05, when there was negative sales growth for these companies due to the uncertainties over the implementation of value-added tax. While Kare and GAPL record negative sales growth for most of the years considered, Toyo and Merit have achieved marginal but consistent rise in sales over the period.

Profits after tax are shown in Table 11.

Table 11

Comparative trends in Profits after tax (in lakh Rs.)

Year	Geno	Wallace	Kare	CFL	Toyo	Merit	GAPL
2002-03	16.4	805.50	42.55	127.26	2.07	-1.6	11.15
2003-04	76.5	974.32	30.91	434.14	2.25	1.2	-245.18
2004-05	181.5	585.32	-184.17	90.77	-0.98	0.64	-238.95
2005-06	213.6	867.54	-120.58	85.55	4.79	1.03	-190.92
2006-07	269.9	184.51	-127.79	126.96	2.21	2.50	-189.17

Source: *Company Annual Reports*

Among the companies, the increase in profitability is more consistent in case of Geno Pharmaceuticals. Profitability trend of Wallace and Cosme Farma has been erratic with sharp drop over some years. It is evident that there is an urgent need to bring down the costs at Kare in order to bring about a turnaround in business performance.

The small scale units like Merit and Toyo have survived the competition by engaging in promotional measures, but feel the heat of competition and regulatory norms. They are constrained by resources and opine that there is no level playing field for small scale pharma players. It becomes clear that there is a need for measures from the Government for such small players in particular, to provide support to their marketing, technological and infrastructural efforts. Governmental policies should not stifle but foster the growth of such progressive units as Merit and Toyo. In the case of GAPL, it is clear that there is an urgent need to prune labour and administrative costs and to make the company more market oriented.

Table 12
Ranking of companies in terms of average sales and profitability.

Company	Rank-Sales	Rank-Average Profits
Wallace	1	1
Cosme Farma	2	2
Geno	3	3
Kare	4	6
GAPL	5	7
Toyo	6	4
Merit	7	5

When classified in terms of sales turnover, companies which achieve a sales volume of more than Rs. 50.0 crore are categorized as large industries. Medium sized companies have a sales turnover between Rs. 5.0 – 50.0 crore and small- scale industries less than Rs. 5.0 crore. Following this classification, Geno, Wallace and Cosme Farma are large scale industries, Kare and GAPL are medium scale and Toyo and Merit Pharmaceuticals are small scale enterprises.

Wallace, Cosme Farma and Geno, occupying top positions among the companies in terms of market size and performance, and are also more market oriented in their strategies and policies. Kare, although, ranking high in sales, ranks low on profitability performance because of substantial expenditure on fixed overheads. Toyo and Merit are small companies in terms of size, and need supportive measures from the government, to sustain in the fiercely competitive market place.

VI. CONCLUSIONS AND IMPLICATIONS

Small local pharmaceutical companies find it extremely difficult to face competition as the therapeutic segments to which their products belong are flooded by substitute products of domestic and multinational companies. It becomes clear that the pharmaceutical companies in Goa, especially the smaller ones, face inadequacies of capital, technology and marketing skills and therefore need supportive measures to strengthen their niche businesses. Small scale pharmaceutical units require government support to obtain Good Manufacturing Practices (GMP) certification and to upgrade their manufacturing facilities as they are constrained with limited resources. The pharmaceutical industry is cost-intensive and companies are required to spend substantially on technology up gradation and quality control. They are also required to comply with the Good Manufacturing Practices norms and to project themselves as quality conscious and ethical organizations. They have to incur increasing expenditures on sales promotion, in providing salaries and incentives to sales staff and in managing distribution channels. It can therefore be stated that marketing success and business performance of the pharmaceutical companies depends to a large extent on their size, where size is measured in terms of total fixed capital and sales volume. However, all the companies irrespective of size need to improve their production and marketing efficiencies to better their performance.

The Government policies, while effectively regulating the industry, should not impede the growth prospects of this industry. Given the low profitability margins, especially of the small industry, the Government should evolve a price and competition policy aimed at the survival and growth of the indigenous pharmaceutical manufacturers. The infrastructural and technological base of the small industries in the group do not provide them a level playing field vis-a –vis large companies and hence it is necessary to provide tax concessions, technological and infrastructural support as well as preference in Government purchase programmes to enable the small players to survive the competition.

References

Borkar, Gitanjali (2004), "Pharma Industry in Goa. Challenges and Issues," GCCI Bulletin Vol. 8. No. 9, Sept.

Chandran, Sajeev; Roy, Archana; Jain, Lokesh (2005), "Implic-ations of New Patent Regime on Indian Pharmaceutical Industry: Challenges and Opportunities," Journal of Intellectual Property Rights, Vol. 10, July 2005. pp. 269-280.

Goa Survey(2009), 'Pharma on a Healthy Growth Curve,' *Business India,* February 22, 2009.

Lalitha, N(2002), "Indian Drug Industry in the WTO Regime," *Economic and Political Weekly*, Vol. XXXVII, No. 34, 3542-3555.

Nair, M.D. (2002), "An Industry in Transition: The Indian Pharmaceutical Industry," *Journal of Intellectual Property Rights,* 7(5), pp 405-415

Panwar, J.S. (1997), *Marketing in the New Era-Combating Competition in a Globalizing Economy*, Sage Publication Inc., New Delhi.

Reekie, Duncan(1971), " Some Problems associated with the Marketing of Ethical Pharmaceutical Products," *Journal of Industrial Economics*

Smarta, B. (1994). *Strategic Pharmaceutical Marketing*, Wheeler Publishing, New Delhi

Smith, Mickey (1983), *Principles of Pharmaceutical Marketing*, Lea and Febigher, USA.

Annual Reports of Companies, Various Years, Registrar of Companies, Panaji- Goa.

8

PROBLEMS OF WOMEN IN SELECTED INDUSTRIES IN INDUSTRIAL ESTATES IN GOA

— Nirmala De Abreu *

I. INTRODUCTION

Women's status and position in Indian society has not been static throughout the ages; rather, various studies have shown that it has fluctuated over the past few centuries. Numerous studies have mentioned the low status accorded to women (Raju, R. (1988), Raka, S. (1985), Singhal, T. (2003)). Indeed, a study has suggested that a woman does not have an identity of her own, and that her identity is wholly defined by her relation to other people (Kakar, S. 1988).Agarwal K. (1988) has put forth the view that women's position in the world has always been subordinate to that of men. Traditionally, women's status and role has been considered inferior as compared to that of men in the home sphere, and this attitude has spilt over to the work sphere. In the labour market women are not taken seriously when it comes to various aspects like cash, training or promotion (Sathy, G. (1991), Lindsay, M. and P. Pattullo. (1977)).

Debi, B. (1988) has inferred that the position of women in the home has improved and elevated in recent years. According to her, women's position has improved to a certain extent, as their contribution to the family purse has helped them in earning both power and authority.

* *Associate Professor, Department of Economics, Govt. College of Arts and Commerce, Pernem, Goa*

The concept of working women is not new. For centuries women have been working alongside men, but only recently have they been entering the labour force in search of work in large numbers. (Singhal, T. (2003), Bullock, S. (1994))

To emphasize the importance of work for a woman, a quote by Jawaharlal Nehru is very relevant. He believes that, "the habit of looking upon marriage as almost a profession, and as the sole economic refuge for women, will have to go before we can have any freedom. Freedom depends on economic conditions even more than the political ones and if the woman is not economically free and self-earning she will have to depend on her husband or someone else and dependents are never free." (Chatterjee, S. A. 1988:146)

Although women occasionally worked, they did so within the four walls of home, as in the past it was considered neither necessary nor advisable for them to leave their homes. It was economic necessity that forced women into the labour market leading to problems like dual role.

II. METHODOLOGY OF THE STUDY

Data for this study was collected from both primary and secondary sources. Primary data was collected through interview schedules. Since the universe for the sampling was not available, two non-probability methods, namely convenience sampling and snowball sampling methods, were used. Secondary data was collected from books and journals. The data has been classified as per industrial estate and gender and tabulated to facilitate analysis.

For this study, 25 percent of the industrial estates were selected. Goa has 18 industrial estates, 2 of which were not functioning at the time of data collection (a functioning industrial estate being defined as one in which the industries were set up and actually producing the desired products). Hence, 4 out of the 16 functioning industrial estates were chosen for the study. These were Tivim industrial estate, Verna industrial estate, Corlim industrial estate and Mapusa industrial estate. From these industrial estates, 5 percent of the functioning industries in each of them were chosen. These industries have comparable proportions of male and female workers. The Tivim industrial estate had 88 functioning industries, and 4 were selected from them. The Verna industrial estate had 104 functioning industries, and 5 were selected from them. The Corlim industrial estate had 60 functioning industries, and 3 were selected from them. The Mapusa industrial estate had 26 functioning industries, and 2 were selected from them for the study. From each of the selected industries, a 10 percent sample of the males and females were considered, as follows:

The data with regard to the total number of workers in the various industries selected for the study in the industrial estate was collected from the Industrial Development Office and from the respondents. From this total, a ten percent sample was selected. Thus, in Tivim, 34 out of the 336 males and 31 out of the 311 females were chosen. In Verna, 17 out of the 169 males and 21 out of the 213 females were chosen. In Corlim, 9 out of the 90 males and 7 out of the 69 females were chosen. In Mapusa, 15 out of the 153 males and 16 out of the 159 females were chosen.

The respondents were interviewed during their free time and not on the factory premises. They were contacted at the bus stops, on the buses, at tea stalls and at their homes wherever possible, so that they were able to give a clear and unbiased picture of their working conditions and the problems faced by them.

III. PROBLEMS FACED BY WOMEN

This section has been divided into two subtopics: problems faced by the women in the place of work and problems faced by the women at home.

Problems faced by women in the workplace include the following: Problems with co-workers - Adverse health effects - Transportation difficulties - Grievance redressal system - Other workplace related issues.

Problems faced by women at home include the following: The dual role problem -Tension due to role conflict - Time spent on managing home/children – Other miscellaneous problems.

The concept of Working Women, has been defined by Vohra, R and Sen, S. K. (1985), in *'Status, Education and Problems of Indian Women Workers'* and this study finds that working women face many problems today in the place of work and at home. These problems differ for the married and unmarried women workers, and it is often seen that these problems are more pronounced in the case of the married workers, most of who are burdened with the dual roles of housekeeper and factory worker.

1. Problems Faced in the Workplace

Problems with co-workers

The relationship of the male and female respondents with the rest of the workers and staff also plays an important role in generating job satisfaction. If the relationship is exploitative and not healthy, the worker will not have job satisfaction and the quality of the work will suffer.

Table 1 (a)
Problems faced by the respondents with male colleagues

	Verna		Tivim		Corlim		Mapusa		Total
	M	F	M	F	M	F	M	F	
No Difficulty	14 (66.7)	13 (54.2)	18 (52.9)	18 (58.1)	4 (44.4)	3 (42.9)	1 (9.1)	1 (7.7)	72 (48.0)
Cooperation	4 (19.0)	7 (29.2)	13 (38.2)	10 (32.3)	5 (55.6)	2 (28.6)	7 (63.6)	7 (53.8)	55 (36.7)
Much advantage	3 (14.3)	2 (8.3)	8 (23.5)	2 (6.4)	4 (44.4)	3 (42.9)	7 (63.6)	9 (69.2)	38 (25.3)
Respect	4 (19.0)	2 (8.3)	8 (23.5)	9 (29.0)	3 (33.3)	3 (42.9)	5 (45.4)	9 (69.2)	43 (28.7)
Harassment seniors	3 (14.3)	9 (37.5)	15 (44.1)	9 (29.0)	2 (22.2)	2 (28.6)	6 (54.5)	8 (61.5)	54 (36.0)
Harassment workers	0	2 (8.3)	6 (17.6)	6 (19.3)	1 (11.1)	2 (28.6)	6 (54.5)	4 (30.8)	27 (18.0)
Total	21	24	34	31	9	7	11	13	150

Source: *Field Survey (Figures in parentheses indicate percentages)*
(Percentage figures may add up to over 100 as multiple answers were permitted to this question)

Table1 (b)
Problems faced by the respondents with female colleagues

	Verna		Tivim		Corlim		Mapusa		Total
	M	F	M	F	M	F	M	F	
No Difficulty	14 (66.7)	13 (54.2)	19 (55.9)	17 (54.8)	4 (44.4)	3 (42.9)	1 (9.1)	1 (7.7)	72 (48.0)
Cooperation	2 (9.5)	8 (33.3)	9 (26.5)	10 (32.3)	3 (33.3)	1 (14.3)	7 (63.6)	2 (15.4)	42 (28.0)
Much advantage	5 (23.8)	1 (4.2)	10 (29.4)	1 (3.2)	3 (33.3)	1 (14.3)	6 (54.5)	8 (61.5)	35 (23.3)
Respect	6 (28.6)	1 (4.2)	6 (17.6)	4 (12.9)	3 (33.3)	1 (14.3)	8 (72.7)	12 (92.3)	41 (27.3)
Harassment seniors	3 (14.3)	5 (20.8)	6 (17.6)	10 (32.3)	4 (44.4)	4 (57.1)	6 (54.5)	7 (53.8)	45 (30.0)
Harassment workers	3 (14.3)	9 (37.5)	5 (14.7)	6 (19.3)	2 (22.2)	2 (28.6)	3 (27.2)	4 (30.8)	34 (22.7)
Total	21	24	34	31	9	7	11	13	150

Source: *Field Survey (Figures in parentheses indicate percentages)*
(Percentage figures may add up to over 100 as multiple answers were permitted to this question)

From the above set of tables the following points emerge:

48.0 percent of the male and female respondents (37 males and 35 females) did not face any problems with the male workers (Table 1(a))

36.7 percent of the male and female respondents have cited lack of cooperation as one of the main difficulties faced by them followed by harassment from senior male officers. (Table 1(a)) 26 females and 29 males face the problem of lack of cooperation while 26 males and 28 females have cited harassment from seniors as a major problem.

39 males and 42 female respondents face the harassment problem hence it was noted that majority of the female respondents face this problem. (Table 1(a))

18.0 percent of the male and female respondents faced harassment from co-workers. (Table.1(a))

48.0 percent of the male and female respondents (38 males and 34 females) did not face any problems with the female workers (Table 1(b))

Harassment from seniors was one of the major problems faced by female workers followed by lack of cooperation. (Table 1(b))

Around 25 percent of the workers complained that both the males and females harassed them. (Table 1(a) and1(b))

Adverse Effects on Health

Working conditions in the factories are far from satisfactory and it is seen that, even the basic facilities are lacking in many cases. Although the respondents seem satisfied with the working conditions, lack of control over these factors and lack of means to change these conditions, might have led to their response that, they are satisfied with them.

Rao, V. R. and Hussain, S. (1991) in their study analysed the effect of the working conditions on the women workers and noted various health problems the women complained of. Headaches, nausea, tiredness, fainting are some of the problems noted by them. These are aggravated due to stress and the summer heat as very often proper working conditions were not provided to the workers. But, it has been pointed out by another study that, the health problems of the women workers are aggravated but not caused by the working conditions found in the factories (ILO (1988))

Table 2
Adverse effects of working in the firm

	Verna		Tivim		Corlim		Mapusa		Total
	M	F	M	F	M	F	M	F	
Yes	0	0	2 (5.9)	0	0	0	0	0	2 (1.3)
No	21 (100)	24 (100)	32 (94.2)	31 (100)	9 (100)	7 (100)	11 (100)	13 (100)	148 (98.7)
Total	21	24	34	31	9	7	11	13	150

Source: *Field Survey (Figures in parentheses indicate percentages)*

Table 2 shows that only two male respondents from Tivim industrial estate replied that they were adversely affected by working in the factory. These two respondents suffered from weaknesses and allergies, but whether these were work related or not, the male respondents could not reply with certainty.

Choudhury, S. N. (1994), in her book *'Employment of Women with special reference to Embroidery Work'*, studied a sample of 250 women from Bhopal with the help of a semi structured interview schedule and case studies. She found that various types of problems such as eye strain, or aches in the neck, back, head and the like were experienced by the women workers.

Gathoskar, S. (1986) conducted her study in the Electronics Export Processing Zone in Santacruz, Bombay and has found that women face many health problems like eye and back strain, headaches ,weakness and ill health. In this study 98.7 percent of the male and female respondents replied that, their health was not adversely affected. Since, the workers in the industrial estates in Goa, were found to be fairly young and recently employed, they might have experienced less adverse effects on health.

Difficulties in Arriving Punctually for Work

Most of the male and female respondents are from rural areas and travel by the local bus. In addition, some of them would have to do household chores before coming to the workplace. Hence, it was necessary to find out whether they faced any problem and difficulties to reach the work place on time, and which were the major contributory factors.

Table 3
Difficulties faced to reach the workplace on time

	Verna	Tivim	Corlim	Mapusa	Total
	F	F	F	F	
Distance	4	12	2	1	19
	(16.7)	(38.7)	(28.6)	(7.7)	(25.3)
Lack of help	2	7	2	1	12
	(8.3)	(22.6)	(28.6)	(7.7)	(16.0)
Inadequate transport	14	10	2	1	27
	(58.3)	(32.3)	(28.6)	(7.7)	(36.0)
No difficulties	7	10	2	11	30
	(29.2)	(32.3)	(28.6)	(84.6)	(40.0)
Total	24	31	7	13	75

Source: *Field Survey (Figures in parentheses indicate percentages)*

(Percentage figures may add up to over 100 as multiple answers were permitted to this question)

From Table 3 the following points can be noted:

1) 40 percent of the female respondents replied that, they did not face any problems to reach the place of work on time. Majority of the female respondents, being unmarried and young, do not

face the problem of dual duties at home before leaving for work. Hence, they reached the place of work on time.

2) 36 percent of the female respondents replied that, it was the lack of transport facilities, which delayed them. Majority of the female respondents came from the rural areas and they did not have regular transport facilities.

3) Around 25 percent of the workers cited distance as the major problem to reach the work place. Since frequent transport facilities directly to the place of work are lacking, the female respondents have to travel by a longer route to the workplace.

Authority to be Approached in Case of Grievance

Every workplace has some grievance, big or small, and every worker faces some grievance with management, food, workplace, workload, etc. This leads to unhappiness, frustration and lack of concentration on the part of the worker. This study tried to find out whether the workers in the various industrial estates also faced grievances in their work environment and the authority to approach in order to solve such grievances.

Table 4

Authority to be approached in case of grievance

	Verna		Tivim		Corlim		Mapusa		Total
	M	F	M	F	M	F	M	F	
Management	5	13	13	16	0	4	1	2	54
	(23.8)	(54.2)	(38.2)	(51.6)		(57.1)	(9.1)	(15.4)	(36.0)
Supervisor	13	11	21	12	9	3	10	11	90
	(61.9)	(45.8)	(61.8)	(38.7)	(100)	(42.9)	(90.9)	(84.6)	(60.0)
No response	3	0	0	3	0	0	0	0	6
	(14.3)			(9.7)					(4.0)
Total	21	24	34	31	9	7	11	13	150

Source: *Field Survey (Figures in parentheses indicate percentages)*

60 percent of respondents replied that they approached the supervisor when they faced any problems, while 36 percent

of respondents approached the management for solving their grievances.

In Goa, it was found that, since the workers faced many problems, major and minor, a hearing of these problems by the right person was very important; as later on these problems could lead to major grievances. Job dissatisfaction is often a result of the non-solving of the problems at the minor scale.

Management Prompt in Redressing Grievances

Along with the right hearing of the problems it is also of equal importance that, the grievance be promptly solved, else it leads to complications later on.

Table 5
Management prompt in solving the problems

	Verna		Tivim		Corlim		Mapusa		Total
	M	F	M	F	M	F	M	F	
Yes	16	18	29	24	9	4	10	9	119
	(76.2)	(75.0)	(85.3)	(77.4)	(100)	(57.1)	(90.9)	(69.2)	(79.3)
No	5	6	5	7	0	3	1	4	31
	(23.8)	(25.0)	(14.7)	(22.6)		(42.9)	(9.1)	(30.8)	(20.7)
Total	21	24	34	31	9	7	11	13	150

Source: *Field Survey (Figures in parentheses indicate percentages)*

Table 5 reveals that 79.3 percent of the respondents were of the opinion that their grievances were settled promptly. This was also supported by the fact that most of the respondents were satisfied with their jobs and the place of work. The young age of the workers coupled with the lack of prior experience and lack of job opportunities could result in their replying that, they were satisfied with the type of jobs they were working in and the conditions in the place of work.

However, 20.7 percent of the respondents replied in the negative. Such neglect of the problems leads to dissatisfaction of the respondents and low levels of productivity and motivation.

Other Workplace Related Issues

The workplace is very important as the worker spends one third of the day there. If there are problems in the workplace, the worker will not be happy and it will lead to dissatisfaction, and will have a major impact on his personal life too.

Table 6 below lists some of the other workplace issues encountered in the survey. From the table the following points may be noted

45.3 percent of the male and female respondents (17 males and 11 females) did not face any problems in the place of work. They found all the facilities satisfactory and did not complain of any lacuna in the working of the factory.

Around 50 percent of the male and female respondents revealed that, they were denied promotions. This includes 36 males and 38 female respondents. An important factor, which has to be taken into account here, is that, many of them are employed in dead end jobs where there are no promotional possibilities. Majority of the male and female respondents are young, with low educational and training levels, hence it may be difficult for the firms to promote them even if there are promotional avenues.

27 male and 23 female respondents have cited lack of training as another important problem faced by them in the work place. Although majority of them did not receive formal training, most of them have been informally trained. Yet, majority of the male and female respondents are of the opinion that, they should receive formal training, as; it would have a positive impact on the quality of their work.

18.6 percent of the male and female respondents cited overwork as a problem faced by them in the place of work. Overwork was due to frequent or occasional additional workload, which was given to the male and female respondents, often without additional monetary compensation.

Table 6
Other workplace related issues

	Verna		Tivim		Corlim		Mapusa		Total
	M	F	M	F	M	F	M	F	
Promotions	6 (28.6)	9 (37.5)	19 (55.9)	17 (54.8)	3 (33.3)	3 (42.9)	8 (72.7)	9 (69.2)	74 (49.3)
Training facilities	4 (19.0)	10 (41.7)	14 (41.2)	14 (45.2)	3 (33.3)	3 (42.9)	6 (54.5)	6 (46.1)	60 (40.0)
Wages	0	6 (25.0)	1 (2.9)	3 (9.7)	0	0	0	0	10 (6.7)
Facilities	0	4 (16.7)	11 (32.3)	5 (16.1)	0	1 (14.3)	0	4 (30.8)	25 (16.7)
Over work	2 (9.5)	2 (8.3)	7 (20.6)	8 (25.8)	2 (22.2)	0	6 (54.5)	1 (7.7)	28 (18.6)
No problems	15 (71.4)	13 (54.2)	12 (35.3)	12 (38.7)	5 (55.6)	4 (57.1)	3 (27.2)	4 (30.8)	68 (45.3)
Total	21	24	34	31	9	7	11	13	150

Source: *Field Survey (Figures in parentheses indicate percentages)*

(Percentage figures may add up to over 100 as multiple answers were permitted to this question)

2. Problems Faced at Home

The Dual Role Problem

Working women play a dual role and hence they often find it difficult to manage both the housework and the factory work.

Nagaich, S. (2001) in her study found that the majority of women do not have much difficulty in managing dual roles, as they spend less time on household duties, since they buy gadgets and have help in performing their house hold duties. Her study finds that working women are more efficient time managers as they have to combine both their house hold and external roles efficiently.

Table 7
Difficulty in managing both home and work

	Verna	Tivim	Corlim	Mapusa	Total
	F	F	F	F	
Yes	5	5	0	3	13
	(20.8)	(16.1)		(23.1)	(17.3)
No	19	26	7	10	62
	(79.2)	(83.9)	(100)	(76.9)	(82.7)
Total	24	31	7	13	75

Source: *Field Survey (Figures in parentheses indicate percentages)*

In the present study, it was found that the majority of the female respondents did not face any difficulties, while only 17.3 percent   of the female respondents found it difficult to manage both the home and the work. This has been shown in Table 7. The unmarried status of majority of the female respondents have resulted in them not facing any difficulty as they do not face the dual burden married women suffer from.

Tensions Due to Role Conflict

Tensions in the place of work and home are common problems faced by the women workers, especially if they have young children.

Table 8 shows that 78.7 percent of the respondents do not face any tensions while performing their dual roles in the home and the factory, as they have help from the family members. Besides, being young and unmarried, majority of them do not have the burden of looking after the young children. The presence of time saving gadgets, too, is very important in saving the women from the kitchen drudgery. 21.3 percent of the female respondents, who have replied that, they are facing tensions while performing the dual role, do not have any help in the housework or are married with children.

Table 8
Tensions faced by the women taking up jobs

	Verna	Tivim	Corlim	Mapusa	Total
	F	F	F	F	
Yes	5 (20.8)	10 (32.3)	0	1 (7.7)	16 (21.3)
No	19 (79.2)	21 (67.7)	7 (100)	12 (92.3)	59 (78.7)
Total	24	31	7	13	75

Source: *Field Survey (Figures in parentheses indicate percentages)*

Time Spent on Managing Home and Children

Time spent on managing the home and children is an important subtopic for the study, as women have to perform dual roles. A woman is responsible for her home and children. Even when there is additional help available the major responsibility is hers. However, since the majority of the female respondents are unmarried, they have not replied to this question.

Table 9 (a)
Time devoted to looking after the children

	Verna	Tivim	Corlim	Mapusa	Total
	F	F	F	F	
< 2 Hours	1 (4.2)	0	0	0	1 (1.3)
2-3 hours	4 (16.7)	3 (9.7)	0	0	7 (9.3)
> 3 hours	1 (4.2)	3 (9.7)	0	0	4 (5.3)
No response	18 (75.0)	25 (80.6)	7 (100)	13 (100)	63 (84.0)
Total	24	31	7	13	75

Source: *Field Survey (Figures in parentheses indicate percentages)*

Table 9 (a) shows that the majority of the married female respondents replied that, they spend more than three hours looking after the children. Since most of the children are more than 5 years, there is no need for anyone to be looking after them the whole day, yet the female respondents have to take care of the studies of the school going children.

Table 9 (b)
Additional help in looking after the children

	Verna	Tivim	Corlim	Mapusa	Total
	F	F	F	F	
Nobody	2	3	0	0	5
	(8.3)	(9.7)			(6.7)
Servant	1	2	0	0	3
	(4.2)	(6.4)			(4.0)
Family	3	1	0	0	4
	(12.5)	(3.2)			(5.3)
No response	18	25	7	13	63
	(75.0)	(80.6)	(100)	(100)	(84.0)
Total	24	31	7	13	75

Source: *Field Survey (Figures in parentheses indicate percentages)*

Since the majority of the children was in the age group 5-29 and were going to school or college, there was no need to look after them full time. Table 9 (b) reveals that, 6.7 percent of the female respondents replied that, besides them nobody looked after the children, while in the case of 5.3 percent of the female respondents, family members looked after the children. Only three female respondents had the facility of a servant to look after the children when the respondents were out at work.

Chores Performed in the House

Working women have to handle both work and home simultaneously. The fact that they are responsible for bringing home the much-needed income does not release them from performing the household tasks. They now have to find time to fit all their previous tasks in the new schedule. This often leads them to start their housework early in the morning or continue the work late at night. Fine, B. (1998) in his study expected that, women would be freed from the burden of house hold work, and left to concentrate on the work yielding monetary benefits yet this has not happened. The private sector which was expected to pick up the household work has not succeeded in doing so, leaving the women overburdened. This study, too finds that, women have to perform multiple chores in the home.

Table 10 (a)
Chores performed in the home

	Verna	Tivim	Corlim	Mapusa	Total
	F	F	F	F	
Cooking	18	30	6	11	65
	(75.0)	(96.8)	(85.7)	(84.6)	(86.7)
Clothes	15	25	5	11	56
	(62.5)	(80.6)	(71.4)	(84.6)	(74.7)
Utensils	14	24	3	10	51
	(58.3)	(77.4)	(42.9)	(76.9)	(68.0)
Shopping	22	25	4	9	60
	(91.7)	(80.6)	(57.1)	(69.2)	(80.0)
House	14	20	5	4	43
	(58.3)	(64.5)	(71.4)	(30.8)	(57.3)
Others	1	1	0	0	2
	(4.2)	(3.2)			(2.7)
Total	24	31	7	13	75

Source: *Field Survey (Figures in parentheses indicate percentages)*
(Percentage figures may add up to over 100 as multiple answers were permitted to this question)

Sharma, I. P. (1999) believes that women, irrespective of the class to which they belong, face some common problems. The dual role problem has affects all classes of women and even the professionals are expected to perform their home roles diligently.

The above Table 10(a) shows that, some of the respondents do the entire domestic work as well as the outside factory work. From the table we find that, 86.7 percent of the female respondents do the cooking, while 74.7 percent wash the clothes and 80 percent do the shopping. This has been put forth very clearly by Maitra- Sinha, A. (1993), where she feels that, a working woman has to play manifold roles of cook, accountant, cleaner, teacher and banker all rolled into one. Thus, we find that, taking a job outside the home sphere does not exempt the women, from performing the household chores in the family, which are traditionally associated with women. The above views have also been supported by Ramanamma, A. (1979) and Rao, V.R. and Hussain, S. (1991) in their study.

Other Help in Household Chores

Working women are already doing eight hours work and they are also expected to put in some hours contributing to the work in the home. Rao, V.R. and Hussain, S. (1991) in their study has noted that unless there was co-operation from other family members, the house hold tasks were considered to be a burden, and generally it was the female family members who helped in the household tasks.

Here, an attempt was made to find out whether, the working women were expected to work all by themselves without any help from family members or a servant (full- time or part time) or whether they had people at home to help them with the house work.

Table 10 (b)
Other help in household chores

	Verna	Tivim	Corlim	Mapusa	Total
	F	F	F	F	
No-one else	3 (12.5)	7 (22.6)	1 (14.3)	2 (15.4)	13 (17.3)
Family	20 (83.3)	22 (71.0)	6 (85.7)	11 (84.6)	59 (78.7)
Full-time servant	0	1 (3.2)	0	0	1 (1.3)
Part-time servant	1 (4.2)	1 (3.2)	0	0	2 (2.7)
Total	24	31	7	13	75

Source: *Field Survey (Figures in parentheses indicate percentages)*

Table 10 (b) reveals that, 17.3 percent of the respondents replied that they do the work alone. Only three respondents had the facility of a servant out of which one respondent had a full time servant. The women who were employed in better paying jobs were in a position to hire servants to help them in household chores and looking after the children. 78.7 percent of the respondents had help from their families in doing the household chores.

Sufficient Time Devoted for all the Work

Since the respondents were women, who worked in the home and in the place of work, enquiry was made as to whether they felt that they devoted sufficient time for her house hold chores.

Table 11
Sufficient time devoted for all the work

	Verna	Tivim	Corlim	Mapusa	Total
	F	F	F	F	
Always	10	17	0	7	34
	(41.7)	(54.8)		(53.8)	(45.3)
Occasionally	11	11	6	6	34
	(45.8)	(35.5)	(85.7)	(46.2)	(45.3)
Never	3	3	1	0	7
	(12.5)	(9.7)	(14.3)		(9.4)
Total	24	31	7	13	75

Source: *Field Survey (Figures in parentheses indicate percentages)*

The above Table 11 shows that 45.3 percent of the female respondents replied that they always had enough time and that they did not face any pressure for completing the work on time; while 45.3 percent replied that, occasionally, they found it difficult to devote enough time for their entire house hold duties. Only 9.4 percent of the female respondents replied that, they did not find sufficient time for household activities. Since majority of the women are young, and have help in the household chores, they do not feel much pressure and tension of completing their work schedule on time.

But, Murty, S. (2001) in her study on 100 working women in Ujjain city in Madhya Pradesh found that, majority of the women feel that, they are not able to pay enough attention to all the household tasks. A large majority of her sample found that the dual role placed a great strain on them. Even the fact that they were going out to work did not relieve them of their family obligations.

Long distance travelling to the place of work and lack of transport facilities has led to time scarcity in the case of women working in Goa. This has also been noted by Srivastava,V. (1978) who finds that a large proportion of the day is spent on work outside the house, leading to scarcity of time for house hold chores. This was in contrast with the full time housewives, in his study, as they could spend a lot of time doing their house hold chores. Her study included 150 educated working women from Chandigarh and a control sample of 150 non-working women.

Satisfied with the Amount of Time Devoted to Housework

Women, who work a double shift, have to find time to fit in all their household chores and very often, the woman might feel that the housework is suffering due to the jobs she holds out of home.

The majority of the respondents, replied that, they were happy with the amount of time they put in daily to complete their household chores. 32.0 percent felt that, the time devoted by them was not enough and that, the household suffered because of their working in the factory. Married women faced this problem. This has been shown in Table 12.

Table 12
Satisfied with the amount of time devoted to house work

	Verna	Tivim	Corlim	Mapusa	Total
	F	F	F	F	
Yes	12 (50.0)	25 (80.6)	6 (85.7)	8 (61.5)	51 (68.0)
No	12 (50.0)	6 (19.4)	1 (14.3)	5 (38.5)	24 (32.0)
Total	24	31	7	13	75

Source: *Field Survey (Figures in parentheses indicate percentages)*

Economic compulsions in many cases contributed to their working in factories, even though they were feeling guilty about neglecting their home. This has also been supported by Srivastava,

V. (1978) who in her study, shows that there are a larger number of labour saving devices bought by the working women and domestic help is employed by them, yet a feeling persists even among the educated women that justice to the family is not being done by them.

Gadgets in the Home

Working women have to do a lot of drudgery work at home and if they do not have some modern gadgets to help them in the work. It is very difficult for them to manage the home and work. This has been shown by Pore (1991). In her study she found that, around half of her sample of women workers, in the garment and electronics industry in Thane and Pune, did not have kitchen aids such as cooking gas, pressure cooker, mixers or refrigerators. More than a quarter of the women workers did all the domestic work without help from servants or relatives.

In Goa, the working women have the facility of gadgets as can be seen from Table 13, and hence the drudgery of the work is considerably less. Besides, 78.7 percent of the respondents have help from the family (shown in Table 10 (b)) and this also helps to reduce the strain on them.

Table 13
Gadgets in the home

	Verna		Tivim		Corlim		Mapusa		Total
	M	F	M	F	M	F	M	F	
Refrigerator	4 (19.0)	6 (25.0)	15 (44.1)	12 (38.7)	3 (33.3)	6 (85.7)	1 (9.1)	9 (69.2)	56 (37.3)
Electric stove	0	2 (8.3)	2 (5.8)	5 (16.1)	0	0	0	0	9 (6.0)
Gas	19 (90.4)	19 (79.2)	31 (91.2)	18 (58.1)	9 (100)	7 (100)	11 (100)	13 (100)	127 (84.7)
Mixer/ Grinder	17 (80.9)	18 (75.0)	23 (67.6)	23 (74.2)	7 (77.8)	2 (28.6)	9 (81.8)	13 (100)	112 (74.7)
Pressure cooker	21 (100)	22 (91.7)	33 (97.1)	29 (93.5)	3 (33.3)	6 (85.7)	10 (90.9)	8 (61.5)	132 (88.0)
Washing machine	6 (28.6)	1 (4.1)	10 (29.4)	5 (16.1)	1 (11.1)	0	0	2 (15.3)	25 (16.7)
Electric iron	12 (57.1)	18 (75.0)	22 (64.7)	26 (83.9)	6 (66.7)	6 (85.7)	9 (81.8)	12 (92.3)	111 (74.0)
Others	0	1 (4.1)	0	1 (3.2)	0	0	0	0	2 (1.3)
Total	21	24	34	31	9	7	11	13	150

Source: *Field Survey (Figures in parentheses indicate percentages)*
(Percentage figures may add up to over 100 as multiple answers were permitted to this question)

From Table 13, the following can be noted:

1) 88.0 percent of zthe female respondents have a pressure cooker. This is important as it saves time for cooking.

2) 84.7 percent of the female respondents had gas facilities. Even in the rural areas, people prefer to use gas as it aids in cooking the food much faster, leaving the working women with more leisure time, or time which they can devote for some other activities.

3) Mixer /grinder and iron were the next set of items owned by majority of them.

4)   All the above items were cheap, so the respondents, even with poor backgrounds could afford them. 37.3 percent of the female respondents had a refrigerator, while the number of female respondents with a washing machine was 16.7 percent. These items being expensive were not affordable to majority of the respondents.

Employment a Right Decision for Women

Women work for many reasons, economic as well as non-economic. Yet, some of the respondents felt that, the decision of the women to work was not a correct one. According to them, a working woman, tends to neglect her family and does not pay enough attention to the children. Table 14 shows that, 22.7 percent of the respondents felt that a woman should not work out of the house but should stay at home and look after the well being of her family. 77.3 percent   of the respondents believe that, working is a right decision and that the woman should be allowed to work; as it makes her independent, gives her authority and puts money in her hands so that, she does not remain dependent on the rest of the family for her needs.

Table 14
Employment a right decision

	Verna		Tivim		Corlim		Mapusa		Total
	M	F	M	F	M	F	M	F	
Yes	19	20	21	26	6	7	7	10	116
	(90.5)	(83.3)	(61.8)	(83.8)	(66.7)	(100)	(63.7)	(76.9)	(77.3)
No	2	4	13	5	3	0	4	3	34
	(9.5)	(16.7)	(38.2)	(16.2)	(33.3)		(36.3)	(23.1)	(22.7)
Total	21	24	34	31	9	7	11	13	150

Source: *Field Survey (Figures in parentheses indicate percentages)*

Both the males and the female respondents were asked whether or not they felt that, the women should work and it was found that, majority of the respondents, both male and female, believe that, women should work and help to support the family.

Since, majority of the respondents are in the young age group, they have the modern outlook, where women are considered largely as important.

This has been supported by Chaudhary, R.K (1988) who in her study titled *'Changing Values Among Young Women'*, conducted in Patna university, where a sample of 260 students were interviewed with the help of an interview schedule, finds that, her respondents believe that, a woman should work and continue to work even after marriage.

Goa is a state, which had the Portuguese influence and so many of the males are prepared to accept females working out of the house. In fact, a working female is one of the criteria when looking for a bride. Hence, women, feel that, working is a right decision, as; it will be an additional qualification when they decide to get married. The rising cost of living too, has led to many families believing that, working female is a boon, as; it helps to reduce the burden of running the household, with the salary of the males only.

Participation in Recreational Activities

Recreation is important to keep the person healthy, motivated and happy. The table below analyses whether the respondents are participating in various recreational activities. Table 15 reveals that 92 percent of the female respondents did not take part in any recreational activity, while only 8 percent of the female respondents took part in various activities such as drama, singing, reading etc. This shows that, leisure activities are very low on the schedule of the workers. They feel guilty if they go home and spend their time on leisure activities when there are household chores to be done.

Ramanamma, A. (1979) in her study has concluded that women perform conflicting dual roles leading to stress and stains due to the lack of leisure time available to them as a result of their house work and office work both of which are not complementary to each other

This has also been borne out in Table 15 that women have no leisure time due to the dual roles played by them.

Table 15
Participation in recreational activities

	Verna		Tivim		Corlim		Mapusa		Total
	M	F	M	F	M	F	M	F	
Yes	2 (9.5)	2 (8.3)	4 (11.8)	3 (9.7)	0	0	0	1 (7.7)	12 (8.0)
No	19 (90.5)	22 (91.7)	30 (88.2)	28 (90.3)	9 (100)	7 (100)	11 (100)	12 (92.3)	138 (92.0)
Total	21	24	34	31	9	7	11	13	150

Source: *Field Survey (Figures in parentheses indicate percentages)*

IV. SUMMARY

This study analyzed the problems faced by women in the place of work and in the home. Women are found to be burdened with multiple roles and problems and to make a study of the various problems; several questions were asked and analyzed. The main learning's are given below: -

1) Majority of the working women replied that, they were not adversely affected by working in the firm in the form of weaknesses or allergies suffered by them.

2) Majority of the respondents cited, lack of transport as one of their major problems to reach the workplace on time.

3) Lack of cooperation and harassment from seniors were found to be the main problems faced in the place of work with colleagues.

4) Lack of promotion, lack of training facilities and overwork were some of the major problems faced by them in the place of work.

5) Majority of the respondents could approach the supervisor in case of any grievance and majority of the respondents replied that, their grievances were promptly attended to.

6) Majority of the respondents are of the opinion that, a woman should work as it leads to financial independence for her.

7) Majority of the respondents did not face any difficulties and tensions while attending to their home and outside work.

8) Majority of the married respondents devoted around three hours for looking after their children and besides family members majority of them did not have anyone to attend to the work of the children.

9) Various household chores such as cooking, washing and shopping were performed by the working women and they had help in attending to these chores.

10) Variety of gadgets such as mixer, gas, iron and pressure cooker were owned by the respondents, to lighten the drudgery in the kitchen and the home.

11) Majority of the respondents are satisfied with the time devoted by them in the house for the household work and an overwhelming majority of the respondents are found not to be participating in any recreational activity.

From the above we can see that, the working women still are faced with many problems and in the selected industries in the industrial estates of Goa we find that, some of the problems are similar to those faced by women all over. Problems in the place of work are common and the women workers are hard hit as they have to do all the work without complaining

V. CONCLUSIONS

The most important causes of concern for working women include problems at the workplace, primarily harassment, problems with seniors and overwork. Inadequate training and indoctrination is also a source of some dissatisfaction. Another factor, which needs to be addressed, is the paucity of adequate transportation facilities. Since many of the working women are dependent on public transport for their daily travel to and from the workplace, lack of proper transportation creates much inconvenience for them.

Turning to the scenario of problems faced at home, the study indicates that working women in Goa have experienced relatively few problems and tensions due to the dual responsibility of family and work. This is largely, due to the fact that, most of them are young and single. In the case of respondents with children, though, it was observed that, they have to spend a lot of time taking care of the children and thus they do carry a heavy burden. In most cases, the women also had help (mainly from family) in the daily chores, and consequently had little difficulty with time management to complete their duties.

References

Agarwal, K. 1988. Status and role of middle class educated earning women in the Indian family. In *Women and Work in Indian Society,* ed. T.M. Dak. Delhi: Discovery Publishing House.

Bullock, S. 1994. *Women and work.* London: Zed Books Ltd.

Chatterjee, S.A. 1988. *The Indian women's search for an identity.* New Delhi: Vikas Publishing House.

Choudhury, R.K. 1989. Supply of work efforts by women in India.In *Women's Contribution to India's Economic and Social Development,* ed. V.S. Mahajan. New Delhi: Deep and Deep Publications.

Chaudhary, S.N.1994. *Employment of women with special reference to embroidery work.* New Delhi: Deep and Deep Publications.

Debi, B. 1998. *Middle class working women of Calcutta.* Anthropological Survey of India. Calcutta: Ministry of Human Resource Development.

Fine, B. 1998. *Labour market theory: A constructive assessment.* London: Rutledge.

Gathoskar, S. 1986 Free trade zones: Pitting women against women. *Economic and Political Weekly.*21(34): 1489-1492.

ILO 1988 . *Women workers in multinational enterprises in developing countries.* Geneva: ILO.

Kakar, S. 1988. Feminine identity in India. In *Women in Indian Society – A Reader.* Ed. R. Ghadially. New Delhi: Sage Publications.

Lindsay, M. And P. Pattullo. 1977. *Women at work.* London: Tavistork Publications.

Maitra-Sinha, A. 1993.*Women in a changing society.* New Delhi: Ashish Publishing House.

Murty, S. (2001) Problems of employed educated women in a few sectors of Indian economy. In *Women and Employment.* Ed. S. Murty. Jaipur: R.B.S.A. Publishers

Nagaich, S.(2001) Women's employment and family life. In *Women and Employment.* Ed. S. Murty. Jaipur: R.B.S.A. Publishers

Pore, K. 1991.Women at work- A secondary line of operation.In *Indian Women in a Challenging Industrial Scenario,* ed. N. Banerjee. New Delhi: Sage Publications.

Raju, R. 1988. *Status of women: A case study of rural and tribal women in Karnataka.* Poona: Dastane Ramchandra and Co.

Raka, S.1985 .*Indian women today.* Delhi: Cosmo Publications.

Ramanamma, A. 1979. *Graduate employed women in an urban setting.* Poona: DastaneRamchandra and Company.

Rao, V.R. and S. Hussain. 1991. Invisible hards-The women behind India's export earnings. In *Indian Women in a Challenging Industrial Scenario*, ed. N. Banerjee. New Delhi: Sage Publications.

Sathy. G. 1991. Work culture of professional women. *Kerala Sociologist.* 19(1): 76-78.

Sharma, I.P.1998. Harnessing human resource potential.In *Human Resource Development*, ed. P.P Arya and B.B Tandon. New Delhi: Deep and Deep Publication.

Singhal, T. 2003. *Working women and family.* Jaipur: R.B. S. A. Publishers.

Srivastava, V. 1978.*Employment of educated married women in India.* New Delhi: National Publishing House.

Vohra, R. and A.K.Sen. 1989. *Status, education and problems of Indian women workers*. Delhi: Akshat Publications.

Our Other Publications

■ **Environment & Development Goa at Crossroads**
Sangeeta M Sonak,Pb,Rs.499, 188 pages,ISBN 978-93-80837-91-8

■ **The Magical Newspaper and Other Stories**
Aumkar Kishore Shah,Pb,Rs.199,92 pages,ISBN 978-93-80837-90-1

■ **364 days of Transformation !**
Kishore M Shah,Pb,Rs.395,159 pages,
ISBN 978-93-80837-89-5

■ **Family and Succession Law in the Portuguese Civil Code of 1867: A 21st Century Approach**
Legal Cooperation Institute Faculty of Law,of the University of Lisbon,Hb,Rs.1500,
514 pages,ISBN 978-93-80837-87-1

■ **Gusmat** Sandesh Prabhudesai,Pb,
Rs.250, 269 pages,
ISBN 978-93-80837-86-4

■ **Clear Cut**
Sandesh Prabhudesai,Pb,Rs.199,
198 pages,ISBN 978-93-80837-85-7

■ **The Jewish Martyrs of Old Goa**
Ivar Fjeld,Hb,Rs.199,84 pages,
ISBN 978-93-80837-84-0

■ **Shell Windows, Short Stories from Goa** Fandacao Oriente-Goa.,Pb,Rs.195, 192 pages,ISBN 978-93-80837-83-3

■ **Portuguese Citizenship of Persons Born in the Erstwhile "Estado Da India' and of their Descendants**
Ave Cleto Afonso,Hb,Rs.1200.
406 pages,ISBN 978-93-80837-82-6

■ **O Vaticino do Swarga**
Ave Cleto Afonso, Pb,Rs.999.
226 pages, ISBN 978-93-80837-81-9

■ **Business Economics (Macro)**
Dr Vaman R Naik,Pb,Rs.200.160 pages,
ISBN 978-93-80837-78-9

■ **Friend Fluence**
Dr. U. G. Borad,Pb,Rs.399.248 pages,
ISBN 978-93-80837-77-2

■ **Get the Truth in 5 minutes**
Dr. U.G.Barad, Pb, Rs.199,144 pages,
ISBN 978-93-80837-75-8

■ **Taan - Tannav Mukti**
Dr, U. G. Barad.,Pb,Rs.99,86 pages
ISBN 978-93-80837-74-1

■ **Lokakaden Vevhar Karpachi Kala**
Dr, U. G. Barad, Pb,Rs.75,45 pages,
ISBN 978-93-80837-73-4

■ **Achatan Manachi Shakti**
Dr. U.G. Borad, Pb,Rs.150,130 pages,
ISBN 978-93-80837-72-7

■ **The Power of Concentration**
Dr. U.G. Barad, Pb,Rs.125,182 pages,
ISBN 978-93-80837-71-0

■ **Beyond Positive Thinking**
Dr. U. G. Barad, Pb,Rs.199,162 pages,
ISBN 978-93-80837-70-3

■ **Small talks! Big Results!!**
Dr. U. G. Borad, Pb,Rs.125,176 pages,
ISBN 978-93-80837-69-7

■ **The Goodness of 10 Nutritions Foods** Dr. U. G. Barad, Pb,Rs.399,
300 pages, ISBN 978-93-80837-68-0

■ **The 80/20 Rule** Dr. U. G. Barad,
Pb, Rs.399, 264 pages,
ISBN 978-93-80837-67-3

■ **Glimpses of Goa's Cultural Heritage** Bhiva P. Parab, Pb,Rs.75,
50 pages, ISBN 978-93-80837-66-6

■ **A Revolt of the Natives of Goa 1787**
Celsa Pinto, Pb,Rs.250,196 pages,
ISBN 978-93-80837-65-9

■ **Business Economics (Macro)**
Dr. Vaman R. Naik, Pb,Rs.200,
160 pages, ISBN 978-93-80837-64-2

■ **Cobos Sopa**
Willy Goes, Pb,Rs.150,150 pages,
ISBN 978-93-80837-63-5

■ **New Light on Ramayana**
Raghupati Bhatt, Pb,Rs.150,100 pages,
ISBN 978-93-80837-62-8

■ **Matanhy Saldanha**
Santosh Sawant wadkar, Pb,Rs.595,
342 pages, ISBN 978-93-80837-61-1

■ **Err, Ere, Ire** Dinesh Patel, Pb,Rs.199,
198 pages,ISBN 978-93-80837-60-4

■ **Indian Jackpot** Dinesh Patel,Pb,
Rs.499,172 pages,
ISBN 978-93-80837-59-8

■ **Goa Administration and economy before and after 1962** Dr. J. C. Imeida,
Hb, Rs.1200, 594 pages,
ISBN 978-93-80837-58-1

■ **Adventures of a Neapolitan in Search of Nothing** Giuseppe Alberto,
Pb, Rs.199,224 pages,
ISBN 978-93-80837-57-4

■ **Fundesco Oriente (dictionary)**
Aleixo Manuel Costa,Hb, Rs.495,
162 pages, ISBN 978-93-80837-56-7

■ **Eco Culture Goa Paradigm**
Vinayak Khedekar, Pb, Rs.295,
236 pages, ISBN 978-93-80837-55-0

■ **Kornelia's Kitchen – 2**
Kornelia Santoro, Pb, Rs.350,
278 pages, ISBN 978-93-80837-54-3

■ **1961 Umbra of Disillusion**
Dinesh Patel, Pb, Rs.199,
200 pages ISBN 978-93-80837-52-9

■ **M.E.S. Emerging trends in Entrepreneurship** Ms. Savia Mendes,
Pb,Rs.350,354 pages,
ISBN 978-93-80837-51-2

■ **You and your Difficult Time**
Dr. U.G. Barad, Pb, Rs.99,106 pages,
ISBN 978-93-80837-50-5

■ **Body language**
Dr. U.G. Barad, Pb, Rs.295, 314 pages,
ISBN 978-93-80837-49-9

■ **Accelerate Reading** Dr. Barad,
Pb,Rs.295, 190 pages,
ISBN 978-93-80837-48-2

■ **Frescoes in the Womb**
Isebel Santa Rita Vas, Pb, Rs.395,
356 pages, ISBN 978-93-80837-46-8

■ **How he met me and other Story**
M. A. Chacko, Pb, Rs.250, 232 pages,
ISBN 978-93-80837-45-1

■ **A Bompy Ride** Trophy D'Souza,
Pb, Rs.299, 202 pages,
ISBN 978-93-80837-44-4

■ **An Unknown Face** Anmol Rathore,
Hp, Rs.150,48 pages,
ISBN 978-93-80837-43-7

■ **A Woman's Guide to Sensible Eating**
Rohini Diniz, Pb,Rs.250, 190 pages,,
ISBN 978-93-80837-42-0

■ **Chaos** Vivek Nayak, Pb, Rs.350,
348 pages, ISBN 978-93-80837-41-3

■ **Choose Your Own Career**
Basil D'Cunha, Pb, Rs.199, 294 pages,
ISBN 978-93-80837-40-6

■ **Ocean of memories**
Mukund Narvenkar, Pb,Rs.199,
180 pages **ISBN** 978-93-80837-39-0

■ **Marine Fungi of India**
B. D. Borse , D. J. Bhat, K. N. Borse,
A.R. Tuwar, N. S. Pawar, Hb, Rs.1995,
486 pages, **ISBN** 978-93-80837-38-3

■ **Operation Vinay** Shrikant Ramani,
Hb, Rs.495, 402 pages,
ISBN 978-93-80837-37-6

■ **Epistermology Search for Truth in
Made Easy** Antonio Rodrigues,
Pb,Rs.150,186 pages
ISBN 978-93-80837-36-9

■ **Being a Goan Christian**
Victor Ferrao, Pb, Rs.195,120 pages,
ISBN 978-93-80837-35-2

■ **Goa Rewound**
Alexzndre Moniz Barbosa, Pb,Rs.195,
164 pages, **ISBN** 978-93-80837-34-5

■ **Infinite Articulation** Perin Ilavia,
Hb, Rs.495,82 pages,
ISBN 978-93-80837-33-8

■ **Principal of Physiology for
students of Medical Science**
Dr. Ramesh A. Dhume, Hb, Rs.995,
458 pages,**ISBN** 978-93-80837-32-1

■ **Kadamba of Goa Inscription**
S.G. Kadamb,HB, Rs.1200, 562 pages,
ISBN 978-93-80837-31-4

■ **Friendsbip Factor** Dr. U.G. Barad,
Pb, Rs.395,368 pages,
ISBN 978-93-80837-30-7

■ **Take Control Diabetes**
Dr. U.G. Barad, Pb, Rs.295, 265 pages,
ISBN 978-93-80837-29-1

■ **Inhuman** Vivek Nayak, Pb, Rs.495,
496 pages, **ISBN** 978-93-80837-28-4

■ **Will Bombay be at Peace**
Pradosh Karapurakar, Pb,Rs.195,
218 pages, **ISBN** 978-93-80837-27-7

■ **Goa Traffic** Marissa De Luna,
Pb, Rs.350, 260 pages,
ISBN 978-93-80837-26-0

■ **Hansun, khelun Xikum-ia**
Pratap Naik, Pb, Rs.110, 50 pages,
ISBN 978-93-80837-25-3

■ **English Konkani dictionary**
Angelus Francis Xavier Maffei,
Hb, Rs.695, 546 pages,
ISBN 978-93-80837-23-0

■ **Veni, Vidi,... Goa Travelers Views of
Goa ancient & modern**
Luis S. R. Vas, Pb, Rs.295, 356 pages,
ISBN 978-93-80837-22-2

■ **Konkani – Italiano Italian-Konkani
dictionary** Ave Cleto Afonso,
Hb, Rs.995, 398 pages,
ISBN 978-93-80837-21-5

■ **The Parish Churches of Goa**
Jose Lourenco, Pb, Rs.595, 220 pages,
ISBN 978-93-80837-19-2

■ **Goa Waits for You** Timesh Kalra,
Pb, Rs.495, 136 pages,
ISBN 978-93-80837-18-5

■ **Inside out** Dr. U. G. Barad,
Pb, Rs.495, 406 pages,
ISBN 978-93-80837-17-8

■ **English-Konkani Dictionary**
Angelus F.X. Meffei, Hb, Rs.695,
545 pages, **ISBN** 978-93-80837-16-1

■ **Understanding Mahabharata**
Raghupati Bhatt, Pb, Rs.195, 146 pages,
ISBN 978-93-80837-15-4